OSPREY AIRCRAFT OF THE ACES • 14

# P-38 Lightning Aces of the Pacific and CBI

SERIES EDITOR: TONY HOLMES

OSPREY AIRCRAFT OF THE ACES • 14

# P-38 Lightning Aces of the Pacific and CBI

## John Stanaway

OSPREY
AEROSPACE

First published in Great Britain in 1997
by Osprey, an imprint of Reed Consumer Books Limited
Michelin House, 81 Fulham Road,
London SW3 6RB
and Auckland, Melbourne, Singapore and Toronto

ISBN 1 85532 633 7

Edited by Tony Holmes
Page design by TT Designs, T & S Truscott

Cover Artwork by Iain Wyllie
Aircraft Profiles by Tom Tullis
Figure Artwork by Mike Chappell
Scale Drawings by Mark Styling

Printed in Hong Kong

**Front cover**
Capt Tom McGuire, who had been
CO of the 431st Fighter Squadron
(FS) within the 475th Fighter Group
(FG) for just 17 days when this
action took place on 19 May 1944,
was leading 'Hades Red Flight' on
bomber escort duty to Jefman
Island, north of New Guinea, when
he spotted three Ki-43s and a lone
Ki-44 near Manokwari. Quickly
manoeuvring P-38J-15 *PUDGY III* in
behind the 'Tojo', which was trailing
the trio of 'Oscars', McGuire hit the
Nakajima fighter hard with two
accurate bursts of fire. Sensing the
imminent explosion of his burning
mount, the Japanese pilot wisely
took to his parachute, thus giving his
American victor his 18th kill.
Although May 1944 generally proved
to be a quiet month for aerial
combat in 5th Fighter Command, the
Hollandia-based McGuire had also
destroyed an 'Oscar' just 48 hours
prior to claiming his 'Tojo'
(*cover artwork by Iain Wyllie*)

EDITOR'S NOTE
To make this best-selling series as authoritative as possible, the editor would be
extremely interested in hearing from any individual who may have relevant
photographs, documentation or first-hand experiences relating to the elite
pilots, and their aircraft, of the various theatres of war. Any material used
will be fully credited to its original source. Please write to Tony Holmes at
1 Bradbourne Road, Sevenoaks, Kent, TN13 3PZ, Great Britain.

# CONTENTS

# AUTHOR'S INTRODUCTION

From the time of its introduction into combat in the middle of 1942, the Lockheed P-38 Lightning was the most successful twin-engined single-seat fighter of World War 2. It was used on virtually every front to which the US Army Air Force (USAAF) was committed, even though it was numerically subordinate to most other fighter types.

Greatest successes were enjoyed by the Lockheed fighter in the Pacific and China-Burma-India (CBI) theatres, despite production delivery priorities being granted to Europe in the spirit of the 'Defeat Germany First' policy. There were never more than about 15 squadrons of P-38s in the South and South-west Pacific at any one time, and the CBI used only four squadrons, two of which (the 449th and 459th) saw most of the action experienced by the fighter. Gen George C Kenney, who held command of the Far East Air Forces (comprising the Fifth and Thirteenth Air Forces), was forced to use just a precious few Lightnings until the advent of the European invasion in mid-1944 released enough of these unique fighters to satisfy his operational needs.

The speed, range and firepower of the P-38 made it the fighter of choice for most USAAF pilots fighting in the Solomons, New Guinea and the Philippines. Over 1800 Japanese aircraft fell to the guns of P-38s from the Fifth, Seventh and Thirteenth Air Forces in the Pacific and the Tenth and Fourteenth Air Forces in China and Burma. At war's end, Japanese veterans gave grudging tribute to the P-38 as one of their most formidable foes.

More than 100 pilots scored at least five aerial victories in the P-38 over the Pacific and Asia. The top American aces of the war flew the aircraft with both confidence and a certain affection which sometimes approached fanatical devotion. Every pilot maintains an enthusiasm for his fighter, but the P-38 crews harboured a special feeling for their mount that translated into stunning performances in battle. From the first encounters at the end of 1942 until the P-38 scored the final Fifth Air Force victories in August 1945, those same pilots made the Pacific skies very much their own battleground.

# EARLY OPERATIONS

The first P-38 victories of the war were credited to pilots of the Eleventh Air Force in defence of the Aleutian Islands in the North Pacific. Two Kawanishi flying boats were shot down on 4 August 1942, and this action seemed to signal an end to the Japanese aerial presence in this remote theatre. Subsequent engagements between enemy aircraft and P-38s became exceedingly rare, resulting in fewer than 50 Japanese machines being claimed as destroyed in the area by war's end.

Many more contacts with the Japanese were recorded in the South and South-west Pacific, however, and most of the P-38 aces of the war came from the squadrons of the Fifth and Thirteenth Air Forces. First victories in the South Pacific went to pilots of the 13th Air Force on Guadalcanal when Lightnings of the 339th FS were sent in to reinforce the besieged island in November 1942. On the 18th of that month eight P-38s were escorting B-17s and B-26s attacking Japanese cargo ships off Buin when a number of enemy fighters attempted an intercept. The P-38s engaged the Navy fighters and claimed three Zeros shot down – these were the first Lightning victories scored in the South Pacific.

In December 1942 two pilots who would later contribute much to the historical significance of the P-38 scored their first aerial victories. On the day before Christmas Lt Thomas G Lanphier was flying with the 70th FS as part of an escort for SBD dive-bombers sent to attack Munda when he claimed an intercepting Zero. Four days later his squadron-mate, Lt Rex Barber, downed a G4M 'Betty' bomber in a preview of the mission he and Lanphier would fly to certain glory within the next four months.

Another pilot who would play a crucial role on that mission began scoring with his P-38 in the New Year. Capt John W Mitchell had already claimed three victories in the P-39 Airacobra when he began flying the Lightning with the 339th FS, and his first kill in the new fighter was an A6M 'Rufe', scored on 5 January 1943. He became an ace some 22 days later when his flight intercepted an attacking Japanese force at 20,000 ft over the Russell Islands – Mitchell personally claimed two Ki-43 'Oscar' fighters. On the night of 29 January he successfully effected a night interception and shot down a Japanese bomber over Guadalcanal, followed some four days later by another floatplane, which became his fifth P-38 victory .

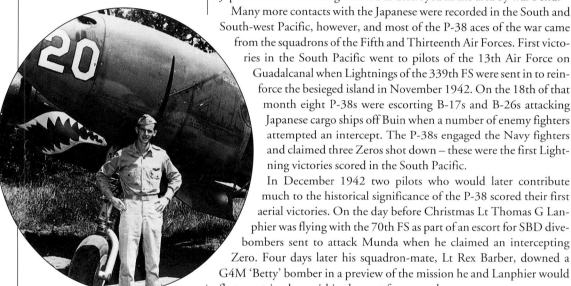

Newly promoted to captain, Curran 'Jack' Jones is seen posing alongside 'his' P-38F-5 (42-12621/'White 20') shortly after the 39th FS converted to the Lockheed fighter in the late summer of 1942. Jones is generally credited with downing 15-victory Navy ace WO Satoshi Yoshino of the Tainan Air Group on 9 June 1942, the latter having attempted to intercept B-26s over Lae in his Zero. This kill was Jones's first, and only, Airacobra victory, his remaining scores being claimed in this very P-38F-5 on 6 January (two 'Oscars') and 3 March (two Zeros during the Battle of the Bismarck Sea) 1943

## P-38 PIONEERS

It was really little more than operational circumstance that saw the 39th FS of the 35th FG become the first P-38 unit in the Fifth Air Force. The unit had been pulled out of the frontline for refit after a difficult tour at Port Moresby in June/July 1942 (the squadron had fared reasonably well in trading ten of their Airacobra fighters for confirmed claims of a similar number of Japanese aircraft) just as a small number of P-38s became available. Having tasted combat in the P-39, pilots of the 39th FS were look-

Charles Gallup scored his premier kill over Dobodura during the first major P-38 engagement in the New Guinea theatre on 27 December 1942. He added two 'Oscars' to his tally on 7 January 1943 over the Lae convoy, followed by a further pair of Nakajima fighters 24 hours later. Gallup's final kill (a 'Betty' bomber) was claimed over Port Moresby on 12 April 1943

Ken Sparks was one of the most exuberent pilots within the 39th FS, scoring 11 confirmed victories before he went home in mid-1943. His first two kills – also claimed on 27 December 1942 – may well have been credited prematurely, as a postwar study of Japanese records shows that no more than five aircraft went missing or were badly damaged on this date. However, Allied soldiers verified his 'Val' claim, having seen an aircraft smoking and diving toward the sea

ing for a machine that would better utilise their aggressive fighting spirit, and were duly offered the P-38 as a replacement for the Bell fighter.

Frontline experience with the photographic version of the P-38 (the F-4) had already indicated that the Lightning promised long range, high speed and enough power to climb or dive away from the Zero. Allied pilots had long since learned to avoid turning in combat with the Japanese naval fighter in deference to its amazing manoeuvrability. Combat in 1942 had shown that for some reason the Japanese preferred to operate at altitudes below 20,000 ft – a fact which suited Allied pilots, whose favoured tactic was to initiate attacks from above in order to capitalise on the superior diving speed of their heavier fighters.

Some of the veterans of the 39th's first combat tour would go on to score heavily with the P-38 from the closing months of 1942 through to the middle of the following year. Lt Thomas J Lynch, who had already secured a reputation as a great combat leader with three confirmed victories in the P-39, would assume command of the 39th after Maj George Prentice went on to lead the new 475th FG during its first months in combat. Capt Charles King was also an Airacobra veteran with the 39th, and he assumed command of the squadron after Lynch was posted back to the United States in September 1943. Lts Richard Suehr and Curran 'Jack' Jones were other 39th veterans who transitioned onto the P-38, and like the previously-mentioned pilots, they too became fighter aces in it.

Despite the subsequent successes of these men, conversion onto the new twin-engined fighter was anything but smooth since few of the pilots, and even fewer groundcrew, had much experience with the highly-advanced P-38. Moreover, mechanical trouble, and problems with assembling the new machines in the field, delayed the Lightning's entry into combat, and frustrated the commanding general of the new Fifth Air Force (as of September 1942), Lt Gen George Kenney. Some help came from new pilots such as future six-kill ace Lt Stanley Andrews and Lt Richard Ira Bong, the latter having been temporarily posted to the 39th from the more experienced 9th FS. Bong would go on to become the ranking American fighter ace of all time.

Prevailing through difficulties, the 39th managed to achieve operational status to the point where it was staging patrols over enemy territory by November 1942. The first aerial victory for the unit's Lightnings was achieved soon after operations commenced when a bomb jettisoned by Lt Robert Faurot landed in the water just off the end of the runway at Lae, New Guinea, and caught a Zero that was taking off in the fountain of water caused by the explosion!

A month later on 27 December, the 39th got what it wanted when a large force of Japanese fighters and dive-bombers attacked the new Allied base at Dobodura, and thus presented the Americans with the chance to at last 'blood' the P-38 in a major aerial engagement. Twelve D3Y 'Val' dive-bombers, a similar number of Zeros from the 582nd Kokutai and 31 Ki-43 'Oscars' of the 11th Sentai were despatched to attack the airfield. The force was spotted by Allied coastwatchers some way off Dobodura, resulting in the alert siren being sounded at Port Moresby's '14-Mile Drome' at about 11.30 am. Twelve P-38s of the 39th were quickly despatched on the 20-minute flight to Dobodura.

Tom Lynch was leading the interception at the head of 'Trapeze Red

Flight' in P-38G-1 42-12715 'White 19', whilst Lts Ken Sparks (in P-38F-5 42-12651) and Dick Bong (flying Lt John 'Shady' Lane's P-38F *Thumper*, alias 42-12644/'White 15') closely followed behind. The flight soon sighted the 'Oscars' and dove in to attack, Lynch quickly claiming two Ki-43s shot down. One of these was apparently blown in half by an accurate burst from the Lightning's formidable armament. Meanwhile, Bong and Sparks became involved with the Zeros, and as a result of their subsequent action reports, each pilot was credited with a single kill. Bong only got a very short burst in at the Zero from just 50 ft away, but was later persuaded to claim the fighter by other observers of the combat. The pair also reportedly destroyed a 'Val' apiece directly over the Dobodura strip.

Other claims for the day included Zeros for Lts Hoyt Eason (in P-38F-5 42-12624/'White 112'), Charles Gallup (in P-38F-5 42-12627/'White 11') and Stanley Andrews (in P-38F-5 42-12659/'White 22') – in total, some 11 confirmed kills and three probables were granted on mostly visual evidence from eyewitnesses. Japanese records admit the loss of two 'Oscars' (Sgt Kurihara got as far as New Britain before he crash-landed and was subsequently picked up by a Japanese naval flying boat, whilst WO Yoshitake failed to return from the mission) and one Zero (which crash-landed back at Rabaul), whilst a 'Val' was listed as missing and another returned to base badly damaged. The only American loss was Ken Sparks's P-38F-5, which was so badly damaged that he had to force-land it on the Dobodura strip.

By the beginning of 1943 the 39th had officially scored some 20 aerial victories, and the squadron was gaining a reputation as the scourge of the Japanese over Lae harbour. Lt Hoyt Eason became the first Lightning ace of the Pacific War over Lae on 31 December 1942 when he was credited with three Zeros shot down (in P-38F-5 42-12653) to add to the pair he claimed on the Dobodura scramble, whilst Ken Sparks again had to force-land his aircraft (P-38F-5 42-12652/'White 33') after colliding with a Japanese fighter during the same engagement – the latter was seen to go down. 'Oscar' pilot Capt Hironoji Shishimoto of the 11th Sentai may well have been the victim of this collision as the Japanese aviator both

**P-38F-5 42-12652/'White 33' exhibits signs of combat damage (right wingtip and trailing edge) after it was damaged in a collision with a Zero on 31 December 1942 – the latter crashed over Lae, being duly credited as the second of two kills scored by Ken Sparks on this sortie. An extremely aggressive pilot who claimed four victories in his first two engagements, Sparks paid a price for his determination as his aircraft was the only one to receive serious damage on both these sorties**

**Hoyt Eason was the first Pacific P-38 pilot to 'make ace' on the Lockheed fighter, but he was soon killed during the Battle of the Bismarck Sea. Forced to ditch his damaged fighter on 3 March 1943, he was seen to escape his sinking P-38 but was never found (*Bong*)**

took to his parachute and subsequently claimed to have destroyed a P-38 during the fight.

On 6 January 1943 the squadron claimed another nine enemy fighters over Lae, two of which were credited to now Capt 'Jack' Jones (flying P-38F-5 42-12621/'White 20'). Dick Bong got two more confirmed over Lae in P-38F-5 42-12624 the very next day, and made ace with his fifth victory over the same area on the 8th (this time flying P-38F-5 42-12653). Incidentally, one of the Japanese Zero units involved in the 7 January fighting over a Lae-bound convoy was the 582nd Kokutai, and one of its pilots, WO Mitsu-o Hori (an ace with 11 victories), was shot down by a 39th FS P-38. He took to his parachute and was picked up by the convoy, but his injuries forced his return to Japan. He later returned to action in defence of the Home Islands in 1944/45.

Dick Suehr also got his fourth confirmed victory on 8 January, and was a first-hand witness to Bong's fifth kill. The former was involved in a head-on attack with a determined 'Oscar' in P-38F-5 42-12627/'White 11' when the concentrated fire from the guns of a Lightning above him blasted the Japanese fighter into bits! Suehr saw the P-38 zoom by at close range and identified it as the aircraft flown by Bong.

By the second week of January the 39th FS had generated five P-38 aces with five or more aerial victories. Hoyt Eason was leading the list of Lightning-only aces with six victories, while Tom Lynch had eight confirmed kills, which included the three he had scored in Airacobras. Dick Bong took his ace status back with him to the 9th FS of the 49th FG on 11 January when he returned to his former unit to help oversee their conversion onto the P-38.

## BATTLE OF THE BISMARCK SEA

Late in January 1943 the 9th FS received 24 P-38Gs that had just been re-assembled and brought up to operational status following their shipment from the US. By February the squadron was staging out of Dobodura on operational patrols, scoring its first victory during the month. At the same time the 80th FS was selected to receive the first P-38s assigned to the 8th FG. For this unit (later to be known by the sobriquet of 'The Head-hunters') it was a matter of good fortune to be picked for conversion onto Lightnings following a spell of misfortune, as the P-39-equipped squadron had recently lost its operational status as a result of a chronic outbreak of malaria and Dengue fever. Headquarters Fifth Air Force reasoned that the other squadrons (the 35th 'Black Panthers' and 36th 'Flying Fiends') within the group were fit enough to carry on combat duties while the 80th both recuperated and transitioned onto the P-38. Great cries of protest were heard from pilots within the 35th and 36th FSs, who considered themselves physically superior to the disease-ridden 80th.

Between January and March 1943 the transitioning unit was replenished with a number of pilots who would go on to achieve considerable success while flying the P-38 with the squadron, including Lts Cyril Homer and Ken Ladd – the former rose to command the 80th, whilst the latter led the 36th FS for six weeks prior to his death on 14 October 1944. Lt Don 'Fibber' McGee had already scored against Japanese aircraft in Airacobras of the 36th FS when he was reassigned to the 80th, and his first reaction upon seeing the 'Flying Bedstead', as the P-38 was sometimes

Paul Stanch claimed his first three victories during the Battle of the Bismarck Sea in early March 1943, rescuing his squadron commander, Maj George Prentice, from attacking Japanese fighters on at least one occasion

called, was that he thought it too big to compete with the more agile Japanese fighters he had encountered in his P-39 days. He quickly learned to use the new fighter to good advantage, however.

Another pilot who moved from the 36th to the 80th was Lt George 'Wheaties' Welch, who had been credited with destroying four Japanese aircraft (possibly two 'Kates', a 'Val' and a Zero) whilst flying a P-40B with the 47th Pursuit Squadron from Wheeler Field during the Pearl Harbor raid. Amazingly, he had gone on to claim three more Japanese aircraft with the 36th FS (flying P-39D-1 41-38359) exactly one year later to become a fully-fledged ace.

Capt Edward 'Porky' Cragg had been with the 80th during its tenure with the Airacobra, and had assumed command of the newly-re-equipped unit in March. Prior to him taking control of the squadron, it had moved to Mareeba, in Australia, in late January to undertake its conversion, although it was not until March that pilots began to arrive at Charters Towers in order to learn the skills necessary to use the P-38 effectively against the Japanese.

Throughout early 1943 Japanese fighter pilots desperately tried to protect convoys of ships that were attempting to keep Lae supplied and reinforced by journeying down from Rabaul, but the appearance of the P-38 seriously hampered their efforts. For example, on 8 January the 39th FS set a single day's record for Japanese aircraft shot down when its pilots claimed 18 in a trio of missions.

During February the Japanese assembled an eight-ship convoy (to be covered by an equal number of destroyers), loaded them up with supplies and 6000 troops, and despatched them to Lae with much haste. The weather was supposed to cover the convoy until it was safely in sight of the New Guinea harbour town, but a B-24 located the ships on the morning of 1 March and a large force of B-17s, B-25s, A-20s and Australian Beaufighters was assembled to meet the hapless vessels 48 hours later.

P-38s of the 39th and 9th FSs would cover the attacking Allied aircraft, and as a result of their employment during this action, the Lightning would secure its reputation as the foremost fighter type ranged against the

Dick Suehr stands by 39th FS combat veteran P-38F-5 42-12654/ 'White' 30, nicknamed *Regina I*. Paul Stanch had used this fighter to damage a 'Betty' off Salamaua on 27 January 1943, before going on to score his first two confirmed victories in it on 3 March. Suehr, however, never tasted success at the controls of this machine (*Suehr via Rocker*)

Japanese in New Guinea. First blood for the 39th came during a day of heavy weather over the convoy when two Japanese fighters were claimed. Capt Charles King (flying P-38G-1 42-12699) got his first confirmed kill when he caught what he identified as an 'Oscar' at the top of a stall climb and shot it down spinning and streaming black smoke into the clouds. Japanese records admit the loss of two Zeros on this date, and these were probably the fighters engaged by the 39th FS.

The next day was to see the pivotal action of the battle, as most of the transports and destroyers were either sunk or disabled. About seven

Zeros and a similar number of 'Oscars' were claimed by the P-38 and P-40 squadrons charged with escorting the bombers, whilst three Lightnings of the 39th were lost with their pilots, including Bob Faurot, who had been credited with the first P-38 victory in the Fifth Air Force, and Hoyt Eason (whilst flying P-38F-5 42-12633), the first Lightning ace in the Pacific. Eason's story had a poignant footnote, for when notice of his death was relayed to his hometown in Mississippi, it was ascertained that the last of his relatives had died while he was in New Guinea, so the town magistrate arranged the necessary affairs for the lost ace.

Despite the loss of a trio of seasoned Lightning pilots, the Battle of the Bismarck Sea was a decisive victory for the P-38 in particular, and the Allies in general. During the next two days the bombers mopped up what was left of the convoy, and the Lighnings of the 9th and 39th claimed even more fighters in the air. Dick Bong scored his sixth confirmed victory on 3 March (and his first in a P-38G) for his premier claim as a 'Flying Knight' of the 9th FS, whilst Tom Lynch got a Zero (the last of six kills scored in his favourite P-38G-1 42-12715) for his ninth victory in total, and Ken Sparks (in P-38G-1 42-12711) was credited with two fighters on 4 March to take his Lightning tally to nine. Lt Paul Stanch (in P-38F-5 42-12654 on the 3rd and P-38F-5 42-12622 on the 4th) tallied three Japanese fighters during the battle for his initial scores, and single victories were awarded to future aces Lts Richard 'Snuffy' Smith (P-38F-5 42-12640), Stanley Andrews (P-38F-5 42-12659/'White 22'), John 'Shady' Lane (P-38F-5 42-12658) and Charles Sullivan (P-38F-5 42-12571). Finally, Capt Curran 'Jack' Jones (in his familiar P-38F-5 42-12621/'White 20) bagged his last two kills of the war (a pair of Zeros) on the 3rd to make ace – he left the unit having completed his frontline tour the following month.

Adm Isoruku Yamamoto, the Chief of the Imperial Japanese Navy Combined Fleet, was frustrated by his inability to move freely within the growing sphere of Allied air power, and was especially alarmed by the fail-

Nicknamed *Thumper*, P-38F-5 42-12644/'White 15' of the 39th FS serves as a backdrop for Tommy Lynch, Dick Suehr and its regular pilot, John 'Shady' Lane, at Port Moresby in late 1942. Lt Dick Bong used this aeroplane on 27 December to claim his first two kills, whilst Lane scored his sixth victory (and a probable) in it on 18 July 1943 (*John Lane*)

ure of the latest convoy to reach Lae. The loss of Guadalcanal in February was a bitter blow to the Japanese, but the threat now posed by Allied air power to Lae, and other strategically important bases nearby, was even more serious. Swift action had to be taken to blunt the impending Allied offensive. Yamamoto had about 350 aircraft (a total made up of both fighters and bombers) at his disposal, which was less than he had commanded during the Pearl Harbor period. Moreover, many of his pilots and crews had seen little combat, as the majority of the experienced veterans of the Hawaiian attack had been lost during the battles around Guadalcanal and, to a lesser extent, New Guinea. Nevertheless, he gathered his forces and initiated *I-Go Sakusen* (*Operation A*), with the intention of destroying the enemy's air power in the region.

The operation began in April and dealt its first heavy blow on the 7th of that month. Guadalcanal was the target, and more than 100 Japanese fighters and bombers were met by 76 Allied interceptors, including 12 P-38s. Thirty-nine Japanese aircraft were claimed for the loss of eight interceptors (one was a P-38), whilst the Japanese survivors in turn claimed forty-one Americans shot down and admitted the loss of twelve fighters and nine bombers. Of importance to American operations in the near future were claims awarded to Tom Lanphier and Rex Barber of three and two Zeros respectively.

New Guinea received its first attacks as part of *I-Go Sakusen* a few days later when 21 bombers and 71 fighters attacked Oro Bay, near Dobodura. The Americans were caught flatfooted and failed in many cases to intercept simply because their fighters were in the wrong place or at the wrong altitude to engage. The Japanese did suffer the loss of four bombers and two fighters, however, a pair of 'Vals' being claimed by Capt Daniel T Roberts (P-38G-15 43-2256) for his first P-38 victories (he had already downed two Zeros whilst flying P-400s the previous August) in an early Lightning operation with the 80th FS – his remaining 10 P-38 kills were scored with the 432nd and 433rd FSs.

On 12 April a large force of Japanese fighters and bombers appeared in the New Guinea skies and was duly met by P-38s from all three operational squadrons then in-theatre. 'Fibber' McGee (in Roberts' P-38G-15 43-2256) shot down a G4M 'Betty' bomber for his first victory with the 80th FS, whilst Lt Grover Fanning of the 9th FS claimed two 'Bettys' and an 'Oscar' in only his first combat! The 39th FS also did well in claiming four bombers and a fighter, Dick Smith (P-38F-5 42-12647), Charles Gallup (P-38F-5 42-12657), Charles Sullivan (P-38F-5 42-12621) and Dick Suehr (P-38F-5 42-12658) scoring the kills, the latter in front of a cheering crowd of thousands of troops at Port Moresby, where his victim crashed into Mt Chamberlain on the outskirts of the town. Having flown 93 missions Suehr was now tour-expired, and he duly returned to the US.

Another six bombers and a fighter fell over Milne Bay two days later during one of the last operations undertaken as part of the ill-fated Japanese offensive. Dick Bong was leading one of the 9th FS flights on a patrol when they intercepted a large formation of bombers. He quickly shot one down (his tenth confirmed victory), but then indiscreetly flew below the formation of 'Bettys' just as they released their ordnance. Bong somehow evaded the falling bombs and went on to damage a second 'Betty', before being chased home by Zero escorts.

# THE YAMAMOTO MISSION

**D**espite *Operation A* being a failure in terms of the human and material cost suffered by the Japanese, it was viewed as having been a success by Adm Yamamoto, who believed that great damage had been caused to the Allies. He now felt sure that their momentum both at sea and in the air had been halted. For example, the Japanese claimed to have sunk ten transports, a cruiser and a destroyer on the 7 April mission to Guadalcanal, but actual Allied losses were limited to one tanker, an American destroyer and an Australian corvette. The Japanese operation did indeed temporarily stall the Allied initiative, but the next few months would see the offensive begin that would not be stopped short of victory in 1945.

Adm Yamamoto used the brief period of inactivity that followed in the wake of *Operation A* to schedule an inspection of forward bases, and to co-ordinate future strategies with his commanders in the field. The admiral was a popular figure with Japanese forces at the front, and his presence would also serve as an added boost to morale. Nobody on the Japanese side could dare predict that a mission hastily plotted just days before Yamamoto's tour would seriously dent that morale for the remaining years of the war.

## DILLINGER

Word had reached the US Navy Department on 14 April through radio intercepts that Yamamoto would make his inspection of forward bases within the next four days. Not for the first time the Japanese code had been broken, and the admiral's agenda was fully known. Secretary of the Navy Frank Knox at first dismissed the information as peripheral intelligence, then reconsidered the possibility of actually intercepting and eliminating one of the key enemy strategists. Preparations had to be intricate not only to camouflage the actual interception, but also to hide the fact that the Allies had access to Japanese encrypted communications. The attacking American fighters (it was quickly determined that only an aerial interception stood a significant chance of success) had to follow a varied route for nearly 400 miles at low altitude to give the impression of a chance encounter on a very long patrol.

**Lt Rex Barber flew Lt Bob Petit's P-38G-13 43-2204/'White 147' *Miss Virginia* on the famous Yamamoto mission, his regular mount having gone unserviceable 24 hours prior to the 18 April 1943 flight. Unofficially at least, the Barber/*Miss Virginia* combination put up an extra-ordinary showing that day, downing both bombers and one of the Zeros launched from Kahili. The official version, which gives him partial credit for both bombers, is still a remarkable record for even as skilled a fighter pilot as Rex Barber (*National Archives via James Lansdale*)**

Surviving members of the Yamamoto mission pose in front of a P-38G reportedly flown by Tom Lanphier soon after *Dillinger*. However, according to official USAF records, the latter pilot was flying P-38G-13 43-2338/'White 122' on 18 April – clearly not this Lightning. Kneeling, from left to right, are William Smith, Doug Canning, Besby Holmes, Rex Barber, John Mitchell, Louis Kittel and Gordon Whittiker. Standing, again from left to right, are Roger Ames, Lawrence Graebner, Tom Lanphier, Delton Goerke, Julius Jacobson, Eldon Stratton, Albert Long and Everett Anglin (*Barber via Henry Sakaida*)

The P-38 was the only possible vehicle to carry out the mission since it had the longest range of any fighter in the South Pacific. Even so, special long-range external fuel tanks were rushed out to Guadalcanal, where members of the 339th FS were being briefed on the planning of the mission. Yamamoto was given the codename *Dillinger* in communications to increase the sinister implications of the project. The planned mission would have all the intrigue of the historical stalking and elimination of the famed American desperado.

Maj John Mitchell was already an ace with five victories in the P-38 (and three others in the P-39) when he was assigned to lead the eighteen fighters selected to complete the mission. Pilots in the attack section included men of the calibre of Capt Thomas Lanphier and Lts Rex Barber and Besbey Holmes, each of whom had scored at least three aerial victories apiece. When two of the eighteen P-38s aborted the mission, four fighters of the attack section and twelve of the covering section would complete the task.

Sixteen P-38s of the 339th FS successfully cleared Guadalcanal before 8 am on 18 April 1943 and set course for the Kahili area, which was more than two hours flying time away along the northern route of the Solomon Islands. To avoid enemy detection in the chain of islands that formed what was called 'The Slot', the P-38s flew to the south-west of the islands out over the sea. Keeping below radar cover, the pilots skimmed over the wave tops in cockpits that were poorly ventilated, and the combination of sun and the new unbaffled external tanks that allowed fuel to slosh freely, throwing the P-38s out of trim with every change of course, made the flight uncomfortable, as well as uncertain.

Maj Mitchell was well up to the task at hand, however, and guided his group of raiders to exactly the right location at the rendezvous time of approximately 9.30 am. Lt Douglas Canning spotted the enemy aircraft (two 'Betty' bombers and six Zero escorts) a few minutes later, and the American formation divided into its pre-briefed attack and covering sections. Four P-38Gs flown by Lanphier, Barber, Holmes and Lt Ray Hine quickly took strike positions above the two 'Betty' bombers, while Mitchell took the rest of the P-38s to a higher level to act as cover in case more Zero escorts appeared.

The next few moments saw all four pilots in the Lightning attack section engage the escort fighters, and both 'Betty' bombers fall to the guns of the Americans. Barber (P-38G-13 43-2204/'White 147') turned in an astounding performance by hitting both bombers and claiming a Zero shot down, whilst Lanphier (P-38G-13 43-2338/'White 122') claimed another fighter and got in shots at Yamamoto's bomber just as it was crashing into the trees having been badly damaged by Barber's attack. Lanphier claimed that he hit the bomber from right angles and fell in behind it just as it lost a wing over the treetops and crashed in flames into the jungle.

At the beginning of the interception the two Japanese bombers had been over the extreme southern coast of Bougainville. Yamamoto's bomber had turned inland while the other 'Betty' headed toward the sea to avoid Barber's attack. The latter lost the bomber when the Japanese pilot skilfully turned beneath his P-38 and headed for the sea, but soon found it again and observed Holmes (P-38G-1LO 42-12690/'White 100') and Hine make quick passes before they were engaged by Zeros. The Mitsubishi bomber had obviously been damaged by the earlier attacks made by Barber and Holmes's flight, and it seemed to explode when it again came under fire by the former.

With both bombers certainly shot down and several Zeros claimed destroyed, the P-38s headed away from what had become a decidedly aroused Japanese airfield at nearby Buin. Despite numerous other Zeros taking off in a forlorn attempt to both protect the admiral and catch the American interlopers, Ray Hine was the only pilot found to be missing when the squadron returned to Guadalcanal.

## CONTROVERSY

Two contentious issues have subsequently arisen in the decades since the Yamamoto mission was successfully completed. The more recent question is one of the morality of selecting an individual enemy personality for assassination. It is well that the issue of morality is raised, but in light of the overwhelming immorality of war, to highlight this isolated action seems almost childish by comparison.

The second point of conjecture is certainly minor, but important in respect to this volume's detailing of P-38 aces. Since the end of World War 2 there has been some confusion about the actual claims of the mission. This is due primarily to the entire action taking place over a period of just four minutes at the most, allied with a lack of camera evidence to provide undisputed proof. Therefore, the only testament to what happened was provided by the participants themselves.

For years after the war the weight of proof came largely from Tom Lanphier, who understandably claimed the major credit for downing Yamamoto's bomber. The USAF carefully weighed all the evidence and wisely decided to divide credit for the mission amongst the pilots of the attack section. Lanphier was given credit for one-half of Yamamoto's bomber and one of the Zero escorts. Barber was given credit for the other half of the kill, as well as a shared credit with Holmes for the second bomber. The latter was also credited with a Zero.

Postwar research located the sole survivor of the six Zeros that escorted Yamamoto's flight, Ken Gi Yanagiya, who reported that the entire Zero escort landed safely after the fight. In light of that evidence it seems that Lanphier's claim of one Zero – certainly from the escort and not from the airstrip at Buin, since that base was only just reacting to the presence of the Americans at that moment – was invalid. In point of fact, as a result of this information, and postwar checks of Japanese loss records, the victory was officially disallowed, leaving Lanphier with a total of 4.5 aerial kills. Up until he died of cancer in San Diego a day short of his 72nd birthday on 26 November 1987, Tom Lanphier sought to be granted full credit for

**Ken Gi Yanagiya during the war. He was the only one of the six Zero pilots that comprised Yamamoto's escort to survive much beyond the end of World War 2 (Sakaida)**

the Yamamoto bomber to maintain his coveted status as a fighter ace.

Other researchers have tried over the years to verify just the opposite by gaining recognition for Rex Barber as the sole victor over Yamamoto, and have presented their case in light of evidence along these major points:

1. Discrepancies in Lanphier's report regarding the Zero and the 'Betty', both of which he stated had lost a wing from his fire. Other pilots on the mission stated that the bomber appeared to have only been hit by tail shots, which is consistent with Barber's account.

2. Testimony from Yanagiya, which goes some way to confirming that the bomber was attacked only from the rear.

3. Physical evidence of the bomber's remains in the jungle of Bougainville, which still carry the bullet holes that were fired from the rear, and the apparent fact that both wings were attached when it crashed in flames.

Aside from the fact that most victory credits are arbitrary in the first place, there is little reason to change the USAF's final decision to grant shared credit. Barber was an exceptional P-38 pilot, and certainly played the major part in the mission, but the Air Force made a wise, and ultimately fair, decision in dividing credit for the mission.

As for the discrepancies in Lanphier's report, from the hundreds of interviews with fighter pilots, and the review of thousands of combat reports filed by those pilots, the author has concluded that honest discrepancies are more the rule than the exception, and Lanphier cannot be blamed for anything more than claiming full credit for the bomber when he deserved no more than half credit. It is probable that he fired wildly from time to time while attacking the 'Betty' at very low altitude, and the last thing he may have observed was Yamamoto's bomber slashing through the jungle – in his excitement he may have confused the large tree branches sliced through by the crashing bomber as a wing shearing away from the stricken aircraft.

A USAF review board disregarded much of Yanagiya's testimony because it conflicted with earlier statements about the air battle, his advancing age, and exposure to a certain line of belief, being cited as factors that may have distorted his memory of 40 to 50 years prior. Another Japanese witness aboard the other 'Betty' bomber seems to confirm the idea that one of the P-38s attacked Yamamoto from the side.

The wreck of the admiral's 'Betty' was examined by the Japanese a few days later, and it was found to be almost completely destroyed in the crash, and resulting fire. Most evidence of bullet and cannon damage had been consumed by fire, and certainly couldn't be considered valid decades later after many years of decomposition in the humid jungle.

Rex Barber made perhaps the most reasoned statement about prolonged dispute of the matter when he declared that there was enough glory for everyone on the mission. At any rate, the real accomplishment was the marvellous job of navigation performed by Mitchell to give the attacking P-38s the best possible chance of completing a very difficult assignment.

# WEWAK, RABAUL AND HOLLANDIA

**D**espite the temporary setback of the *I-Go* offensive of April, the balance of power shifted decisively in favour of the Allies in the Solomons and New Guinea following fierce fighting between May and July 1943. Japanese air attacks lashed out at the eastern end of the latter island in a desperate, but ultimately futile, effort to reverse the growing domination of both air and land forces emanating from Port Moresby. No less troublesome were the ominous signs of Allied expansion from Guadalcanal, for if the enemy could consolidate and expand their bases in this region, then the way to Rabaul would be open and defeat in the area inevitable.

By the beginning of June the US Navy and Marines, Royal New Zealand Air Force and the USAAF's Thirteenth Air Force had begun probing the defences of the upper Solomon Islands, pricking the nerves of the Japanese air and sea forces in the process. On the 7th of the month the Japanese Navy reacted by sending a large number of Zeros to cover a force of 'Val' dive-bombers that had been sent aloft in an obvious effort to draw the enemy into a decisive air battle. The results were claims of 24 Zeros shot down for the loss of five American fighters – Japanese records state that 41 Allied fighters were downed and only nine Zeros lost, with a further five badly damaged.

Three of the Zeros were claimed by two P-38 pilots of the 339th FS. Lts Bill Harris and Murray Shubin were relatively new to the squadron when they engaged part of the Japanese force, but this lack of experience didn't stop the former downing two Mitsubishi fighters and the latter 'bagging' a single kill. Both pilots would emerge victors again in a monumental air battle fought once more over the Allied convoys off Guadalcanal little more than a week later.

The Japanese Navy sent 24 bombers, escorted by 70 Zeros, to attack shipping off Lunga Point on 16 June, but enroute a coastwatcher on Vella Lavella sighted the formation just after noon and warned the defenders on Guadalcanal in time for them to scramble more than 100 interceptors. The Japanese were engaged well before their planned target was reached, and the intercepting fighters reported having destroyed a combined total of 42 Zeros and 'Vals' – Japanese records list 13 'Vals' and 15 Zeros as having failed to return. The P-38s of the

Tom Lynch is seen standing next to 'his' P-38G-1 (42-12859) soon after it had been decorated with his latest victory decal, which denoted a 'Hamp' kill scored on the afternoon of 8 May 1943. His reputation within the 39th FS was legendary, and he was even credited with shooting down a Japanese fighter over Lae whilst flying a Lightning with drop tanks that would not release *(Rosemary Lynch via Norbert Krane)*

339th claimed 11 of the Zeros shot down, with Harris again downing two before his guns jammed, which effectively put him out of action. No such problems afflicted Murray Shubin's P-38G, however.

He was about 50 miles west of Guadalcanal at 29,000 ft, receiving vectoring directions from fighter controllers back at Henderson Field, when a formation of Zeros and 'Vals' was observed about 6000 ft below. With the sun behind him, Shubin (and his flight) were presented with the perfect opportunity to effect a bounce on the Zero cover, and he made the most of it by splitting up the Japanese escorts and sending four of them down in flames.

In the whirling dogfight that followed, one of the P-38s was forced to break off the engagement with a damaged engine, whilst Harris and another pilot left with either jammed or empty guns – this left Shubin to face the enemy fighters alone. Six of the Zeros stayed to offer Shubin combat, and he readily accepted once he realised that the enemy must have been either crazy or inexperienced to have stayed in one group, rather than break up into individual attacking elements. For the next 45 minutes the intrepid P-38 pilot used dive and zoom tactics to attack the rearmost elements of the huddled Japanese gaggle until he finally claimed a total of five confirmed Zeros and one probable going down in flames.

All of these victories were confirmed by a number of witnesses who had observed the astounding fight as it drifted down over the coast of Guadalcanal. With five Zeros confirmed, Shubin became the only P-38 pilot in the Pacific to 'make ace' in a single combat.

### 'FORTRESS WEWAK'

The most formidable Japanese base on New Guinea was the complex at Wewak, situated midway between the Huon peninsula and the last great enemy stronghold of Hollandia, on the north-west coast below the Vogelkop peninsula. It proved possible to neutralise Wewak without immediate invasion, however, thus allowing the Allies to bypass the area until the base was finally captured in May 1945.

The complex of airfields in and around Wewak would soon come under the command of the 4th Air Army of the JAAF, whose fighter units included at least four equipped with 'Oscars' and two others with the temperamental, but still formidable, Ki-61 'Tony'. Additional units included at least one twin-engined fighter (Ki-45 'Nick') sentai, plus other 'Tony' and 'Oscar' units on nearby New Britain – with possible reinforcement by other Army and Navy (Zero) units from bases in the vicinity, Wewak had the potential to oppose any assault.

However, the Allied offensive took on an inexorable momentum with the invasion of New Georgia, in the Solomons, in late June/early July, and the subsequent progression from Nassau Bay to the Lae/Salamaua

Ed 'Porky' Cragg commanded the 80th FS from March 1943 until his death in combat over Cape Gloucester on Boxing Day 1943. Credited with coining the sobriquet 'Headhunters' for 'his' squadron, Cragg scored his first victory (a 'Hap') near Salamaua on 21 May 1943 – he also claimed a second 'Hap' as a probable on this sortie (*Rocker via Ethell*)

Capt Tom Lynch is seen outside the 39th FS's 'hut HQ' at Port Moresby soon after scoring his ninth kill (an 'Oscar') during the Battle of the Bismark Sea on 3 March 1943 (*USAF*)

**Future eight-kill ace Lt John L Jones was generally credited with scoring Fifth Fighter Command's 500th aerial victory on 21 May 1943 when he sent a 'Hap' down in flames into cloud north of Salamaua whilst flying P-38G-15 43-2386. Photographed several months after achieving *the* kill, Jones is seen posing with '386, whose scoreboard also denotes victories scored in it by several other pilots including aces Cy Homer and Ken Ladd (*USAF*)**

**39th FS aces Stanley Andrews, Charles Sullivan (now O'Sullivan) and Tom Lynch show off their new decorations in mid-1943. By the end of May 1943 the latter had ten victories, whilst on 21 July Andrews claimed a 'Tony' and five days later Sullivan an 'Oscar' for their fifth victories respectively**

area. Air strikes covered by P-38s soon began to neutralise bases along the route to Wewak.

On 18 July, whilst escorting transports supporting the invasion, the 39th FS ran into a large force of 'Oscars' around the Salamaua area. 'Shady' Lane (P-38F-5 42-12644) claimed one for his fifth confirmed victory, whilst another was added to his score as a probable. Ken Sparks (P-38G-1 42-12711) plunged into the fray and bagged the only other confirmed kill for his tenth victory – three additional probables and a damaged claim were registered by the remaining six P-38 pilots that took part in the mission. It had already been noted by his superiors that double ace Sparks was both a skilled and somewhat overly brave pilot who disregarded his own safety to get at the enemy. Both were evident in his next combat, which took place just three days later.

Bogadjim – a Japanese base on Astrolabe Bay below Madang and Alexishafen – was the target of a B-25 raid on the 21st. When the 39th reached the combat area with 13 P-38s, they found the 80th FS already engaged in a bitter dogfight with a large number of Japanese fighters. Capt Charles King (P-38F-5 42-12653) was leading the 39th, and he quickly entered the battle, shooting down his second Japanese fighter (a Ki-43) to draw first blood for the squadron.

Paul Stanch (P-38G-5 42-12851) claimed two more 'Oscars' to confirm his ace status, whilst Charles Sullivan (P-38G-15 43-2293) downed a hapless Japanese bomber that had strayed into the engagement to register his own fifth kill. 'Snuffy' Smith (P-38F-5 42-12640) ran into Ki-61 'Tonys' and sent two of them down to become an ace, whilst Stanley Andrews (P-38G-5 42-12859/'White 19') also claimed a Kawasaki fighter for his fifth victory, although he later insisted that the Japanese he had faced was flying a Messerschmitt Bf 109 until his unusually clear P-38 gun film indicated that his quarry was most definitely flying an inline-engined Ki-61. Incidentally, the 39th FS set a record on this mission when its haul of 12 victories made it the first Fifth Fighter Command squadron to score over 100 Japanese kills.

As alluded to earlier, Ken Sparks (P-38G-5 42-12846) was his usual ebullient self in this mission, attacking Japanese aircraft from any angle, and nearly getting himself shot down in the process. He used every advantage his P-38 possessed to escape several vengeful enemy pilots

The 339th FS's Lt Murray 'Jim' Shubin stands by his P-38G-13, nicknamed *Oriole* (43-2242 'White 129'), soon after completing his 'ace in a day' sortie on 16 June 1943. Shubin had earlier claimed two Zeros (a 'Rufe' floatplane on 2 February and a Zeke on 7 June) prior to becoming the sole P-38 pilot in the Pacific to be officially credited with five victories in one combat – he also claimed a probable in this same sortie. All of Shubin's victims on 16 June were Zekes, and they fell between Beaufort Bay and Savo Island, in the Solomon Islands chain. He went on to down two more Zeros on 10 October, followed by a pair of 'Vals' 17 days later. Sadly, Shubin was killed in France in 1956 in a motoring accident after suffering a heart attack whilst at the wheel of his car. He was serving as CO of the 71st Bomb Squadron at the time of his death (*USAF*)

who had undoubtedly witnessed his attack on one of their comrades that had resulted in the latter's 'Oscar' going down in flames after an especially long burst of fire from Sparks' Lightning (nine seconds' worth of firing according to the latter's combat report). After recording his 11th confirmed victory, Sparks remained at odds with some of the leaders of the 39th following his exploits both in the air and on the ground, so he elected to rotate home early, rather than have them subdue his high spirits. Although assigned to the 443rd Base Unit as an instructor early in 1944, Sparks had hoped to continue his combat career with another unit before war's end, but sadly he was killed in a P-38 crash during a training flight off the coast of California.

Wewak received its first major attack on 17 August 1943 when the 9th, 39th and 80th FSs sent their fighters (along with the three new P-38 unit of the 475th FG) to escort B-25s on a surprise low-level raid on Wewak. The raiders succeeded in reaching their target undetected, resulting in dozens of Japanese aircraft being destroyed or damaged on the ground. Not a single fighter got into the air to challenge the American force, and no losses were recorded.

Another raid was scheduled for the following day, and once again six P-38 squadrons would escort the bombers. This time, however, the 475th FG met the enemy in the air, and claimed 15 destroyed for the loss of just a single P-38. Some 16 'Oscars' from the 24th and 59th Sentais, plus five 'Tonys' of the 68th and two 'Nicks' of the 13th rose to meet the Americans. Several of the intercepting fighters were lost, including the Ki-43 of formation leader Nanba Shigeki, which crash-landed on But West airfield – its destruction may have been claimed by as many as four of the P-38 pilots! Future 431st FS aces Capt Verl Jett (P-38H-5 42-66742) and Lts Ed Czarnecki (P-38H-1 42-66502) and Lowell Lutton (P-38H-1 42-66548) each managed to claim pairs of wildly manoeuvring 'Oscars' – these were Czarnecki's first confirmed kills for Lutton had downed a Ki-43 two days earlier, whilst Jett's premier score dated back to 28 December 1942 when he was credited with a solitary kill over a Ki-51 'Sonia' bomber whilst flying a P-39D-1 (41-38396) with the 36th FS.

Another 431st FS pilot who opened his account during this massive dogfight was Lt Francis 'Fran' Lent (P-38H-1 42-66550), the young Minnesotan becoming separated from his flight in the initial turning manoeuvres prior to engaging the enemy. He had wisely attached himself to the element of P-38s that included Lt Tom McGuire (P-38H-1 42-66592/*PUDGY*). Both pilots had to defend each other with some alacrity, and each shot a fighter (McGuire an 'Oscar' and Lent a 'Hap') off the tail of a P-38 in the small formation. McGuire ended the day as top scorer of the day when he got a second Ki-43 and a 'Tony', the latter being literally shot off the tail of a B-25 of the 405th BS – the Mitchell's crew gratefully confirmed the kill for him upon his return to base.

All six P-38 units were back on escort duty during the next strike on Wewak three days later, and again the 475th made impressive claims of more than 20 Japanese interceptors shot down for no losses. They had now downed more than 50 kills in just three missions! McGuire, again flying *PUDGY*, shot down two 'Oscars' and damaged a 'Nick' to become an ace in just his second combat, whilst Frank Lent, who was now flying as the former's wingman (still in 42-66550), also claimed an 'Oscar' and a 'Nick' for his third and fourth victories.

The 432nd FS did almost as well for the 475th FG when it claimed eight Japanese fighters around But on this day, Capt Danny Roberts (P-38H-1 42-66513) – previously with the 80th FS – leading his wingman into a gaggle of six 'Oscars' that had just finished off a P-38 from his former unit and immediately avenging its loss by flaming a Ki-43. He then attacked another 'Oscar', which was seen to crash near the end of the But runway. Future 11-kill ace Lt John Loisel (P-38H-1 42-66537) began his scoring on this mission when he claimed two 'Tonys', whilst fellow 432nd squadron-mate Lt Fred 'Squareloop' Harris (P-38H-1 42-66553) had a remarkable day when he also shot down a pair of Ki-61s and damaged four others. Lt Billy Gresham (P-38H-1 42-66750) was yet another pilot from the squadron to achieve his first victory on 21 August, claiming to have scored the telling hits on a badly mauled 'Nick' that had been attacked by at least four other P-38s – each of the Lightning pilots claimed to have destroyed the twin-engined interceptor!

By this stage Wewak had begun its gradual decline as a major Japanese base in New Guinea, and although it would experience air raids for the rest of the year, its primary value would be reduced to that of an impediment to Allied operations in other areas, rather than as a bastion of defence. Wewak's many AA guns and handful of operational fighters did, however, continue to exact a steady toll of Allied aircraft until they were silenced by invasion in 1945.

One of the pilots who would be

**This publicity photo shows the fifth Japanese flag being stencilled onto the nose of Shubin's P-38 by his suitably proud groundcrew at Guadalcanal (*UPI*)**

affected by Wewak was Tom McGuire. His original *PUDGY* – P-38H-1 42-66592, dubbed with a nickname that McGuire reportedly disliked as it referred to his wife – was taken out of service after receiving cannon damage near Wewak on 29 August 1943. He had just claimed a Zeke and a 'Tony' for his sixth and seventh victories when a third Japanese fighter slipped in unnoticed and badly damaged his Lightning.

Future six-kill ace Lt James Ince of the 432 FS (he had earlier scored his first trio of kills in P-38F-1s and Gs with the 80th FS in May/June 1943) earned the title of 'Impossible Ince' partly because of his experiences over Wewak during a raid on 20 September. He was leading an element within the first flight of P-38s when six aggressively flown 'Tonys' attacked them from the rear. Ince, and several other pilots, immediately turned into their opponents so as to face them head on, but the Ki-61s were undeterred, and through accurate fire quickly registered hits on a number of the Lightnings.

Two of the Kawasaki fighters concentrated on Ince, and he was disheartened to find that neither his 20 mm cannon or quartet of 0.5-in cal Browning machine-guns would fire. Amazingly, bearing in mind the recognised skill of the Japanese pilots engaged in this action, Ince survived their initial pass unscathed and had to pull up over the top of them as they rapidly converged. While he was in the clear for just a brief moment, he tried in vain to recharge his guns, but they simply refused to operate. Meanwhile, the 'Tonys' had rapidly turned back into the defenceless Lightning and were closing fast from the rear. Ince had no choice but to use the superior diving speed of his P-38 to outrun his pursuers. Once back at base, his groundcrew found that a fuse had failed within the electrics that controlled the firing of the armament, thus rendering his guns completely inoperable.

Exactly a week prior to Ince's close shave, fellow 475th FG pilot Lt Vincent Elliott (of the 431st FS) earned his first confirmed victory whilst escorting B-24s sent to bomb 'Fortress Wewak'. Flying as Tom McGuire's wingman, Elliott sensed that he was about to see his first action when he heard that Japanese fighters had been sighted some 12,000 ft below them. With combat in the offing, McGuire attempted to 'punch off' his near-empty external wing tanks but found they would not budge. Realising that he would be little more than a sitting duck should he attempt to engage the highly agile Japanese fighters, a frustrated McGuire instead headed inland, but not before telling Elliott to remain with the flight.

Having temporarily broken away from the remaining members of his squadron to cover his leader whilst the latter attempted to jettison his tanks, Elliott returned to find three 431st P-38s attacking four enemy fighters just below him. Without a moment's hesitation, he dove in after

Six aces of the 339th FS in February 1944. In the back row, from left to right, are Henry Meigs, George Chandler and Truman Barnes, whilst squatting in the front are Bill Harris and Thomas Walker. Harris scored two victories on the same 16 June 1943 mission that saw Shubin 'bag' his five, whilst Meigs 'bagged' three of his six P-38 kills at night whilst flying with the 6th Night Fighter Squadron (*Chandler*)

**Lts Dick Bong and Jerry Johnson were friendly rivals in the 9th FS, and both men scored heavily in the second half of 1943. Indeed, so eager were they to add kills to their respective tallies that on an escort mission in July both pilots radioed astonished B-25 gunners to ask them to stop firing so that they could have a crack at downing the attacking 'Oscar' themselves!**

**As mentioned earlier in this chapter, Lt Stanley Andrews 'made ace' with the 39th FS on 21 July 1943 when he was credited with destroying one of the first Ki-61 'Tonys' encountered by a Fifth Fighter Command pilot. This date was also significant for the fact that the 39th became the first unit in the Pacific to achieve 100 aerial kills. Andrews got his final victory (a Zeke) on 20 August 1943 (*Andrews*)**

them. Thanks to his fighter's superior diving speed, Elliott soon caught up with a Japanese aircraft that he immediately identified as a Zero and fired a 60° deflection shot at it. His aim was good despite the acute angle of the attack, and pieces flew away from the canopy area, followed by a thin stream of white smoke that emanated from the engine and trailed back into the slipstream. The Japanese pilot rolled over slowly and headed straight down, followed closely by Elliott, who trailed the stricken fighter down to about 3000 ft. At this height, and with the Zero still turning over slowly as it headed earthward, Elliott finally considered discretion to be the better part of valour and climbed back up to rejoin Capt John Hood's flight for the return trip to Dobodura.

The 80th FS was also heavily involved in the Wewak operations at this time, with seasoned combat veteran 'Cy' Homer (P-38G-1 42-12705) gaining his fifth victory over the area when he shot down an 'Oscar' during the extensive operations flown on 13 September. His boss, Maj Ed Cragg (in his personal P-38H-1 42-66506/*PORKY II* – he was later lost in this very machine on Boxing Day 1943), had also made ace by downing a Zeke and a 'Tony' over Bogadjim on 20 August, followed by an 'Oscar' 24 hours later (this time in P-38H-1 42-66563). As mentioned earlier, George Welch had already scored seven kills when he was posted to the Lightning-equipped 80th FS, and he too became a P-38 ace during the 20 August Wewak mission when he downed three 'Oscars' in P-38H-1 42-66578.

## NIGHTFIGHTERS

Capt John Mitchell was the pioneer P-38 nightfighter, having unsuccessfully attempted to intercept nocturnal raiders over Guadalcanal as early as January 1943. He and his fellow pilots within the 339th FS had discussed the possibility of using the Lightning, in conjunction with the island's searchlights, to counter the nuisance raids staged almost nightly with virtual impunity by the Japanese bombers. A young 22-year-old New Yorker by the name Henry Meigs, Jr, was one of those who eagerly awaited the chance to attempt a night interception, and like his squadronmates, felt that the American AA batteries posed no serious threat to the P-38 pilots should they open fire whilst an interception was taking place. They reasoned that if the gunners couldn't hit a large, slow, Japanese bombers after months of practice, what chance did they have against the smaller and more agile Lightning!

Eventually, a small detachment of pilots was seconded to the 6th Night Fighter Squadron (NFS), and at about 1.10 am on 15 August 1943 the Lightning pilots were given their big chance. Lt Meigs (flying a P-38G) was scrambled to intercept an incoming 'Betty', which subsequently became caught in the base searchlights and was quickly despatched in flames.

On the night of September 20/21, a larger force of six 'Bettys' of the 702nd Kokutai arrived over Guadalcanal and was quickly caught up in the radar-directed searchlight beams. Meigs was again airborne and attacked without delay, exchanging fire with the tail gunner of one of the 'Bettys'. The latter was soon silenced, but not before he had put a cannon shell through one of the Lightning's elevators. Undaunted by the sudden change in the handling characteristics of his mount, Meigs fired his four .5-in cal machine-guns into the 'Betty's' right wingroot and the Japanese bomber went down in flames.

The searchlights (known colloquially as 'Eveready Senior') soon caught a second 'Betty' in the pattern and Meigs bored in for yet another attack.

This time several of the bomber's gunners let fly at the stalking P-38, and Meigs felt a number of strikes on his fighter. None deflected him from the task at hand, however, and he answered with a full broadside of guns and cannon which quickly sent the doomed 'Betty' to a fiery grave. Lt Henry Meigs went on to score three more daylight victories in P-38Js with the 339th FS in early 1944, thus becoming one of the few Lightning pilots to achieve both day and night kills. After the war he went on to become a judge, and today still practices law in his home state of Kentucky.

## RABAUL – P-38 'ACE MAKER'

With the potential threat of Wewak largely eliminated by the late summer of 1943, there remained only the great Japanese bastion at Rabaul, on New Britain, left to menace Allied advances up the Solomon Islands chain and along the northern coast of New Guinea. Senior commanders realised that an all out invasion of Rabaul would result in a terrible loss of both men and equipment, so alternative plans were drawn up to isolate the base through the employment of similar tactics to those used so successfully against Wewak.

The Japanese had concentrated both their best ground troops and fighter pilots in the area to insure that any advance on Rabaul would exact a heavy price in Allied air and ground forces.

The weather in the region also played into the defender's hands, as towering tropical fronts would suddenly appear to heights in excess of 30,000 ft, making the bomber route from New Guinea or the Solomons to Rabaul extremely perilous – few Allied aircraft could climb over storms that reached that high into the atmosphere, particularly when carrying a hefty bombload.

It was a terrifying prospect for most fighter pilots to consider even flying to Rabaul, but the planned assault involved not only protecting bombers at altitude, but also low-level sweeps that would expose them to AA fire of unusual ferocity – not to mention the aerial opposition put up by some of the best Zero pilots in the Navy. A number of 'Oscar' and 'Tony' units must have also been scattered across smaller airfields on New Britain as combat reports filed by Allied pilots following sorties over Rabaul described encounters with varied types of JAAF fighters.

The Fifth Air Force delivered the first blow against New Britain on 12 October 1943 when P-38s of the 1st Provisional Fighter Squadron escorted B-24s sent to attack the harbour and numerous airfields in the

**Lts Ken Taylor and George Welch were amongst the handful of pilots who managed to get airborne during the attack on Pearl Harbor on 7 December 1941. Flying P-40Bs with the 47th PS, Taylor claimed two attackers and 'Wheaties' Welch four. These were the former's only kills in combat, but exactly a year later Welch downed three more enemy aircraft near Buna in P-39D-1 41-38359 whilst flying with the 36th FS. He went on to claim a further nine kills in P-38s with the 80th FS, including another four in one mission on 2 September 1943, before returning to the USA and joining North American Aviation as a test pilot in 1944. His postwar career saw him perform the first flights for the P-82E Twin Mustang and the F-86 Sabre, but he was killed in a crash at Edwards AFB on 12 October 1954 whilst testing the new F-100 Super Sabre (*Taylor via Lambert*)**

Rabaul area. Simultaneously, B-25s (also with a Lightning escort) struck the same airfields from low-level, whilst 12 Beaufighters of the RAAF's No 30 Sqn strafed Tobera airstrip. In a repeat of the Wewak success of 17 August, almost total surprise was achieved by the raiders, and great destruction of aircraft and other equipment was reported, although again there was little air opposition – only three Japanese aircraft were claimed to have been shot down.

Lt Jim Ince (left) and his P-38H-1 (42-66568/'White 144'), nicknamed *Impossible Ince,* are seen at Dobodura in late 1943. Ince scored two victories with the 80th FS in the spring of 1943 prior to being sent to the newly-formed 475th FG to help fill the ranks of the 432nd FS. He claimed his next two victories whilst defending the Allied invasion convoy off Lae on 22 September 1943, and then completed his scoring two months later with single Zekes on 9 and 16 November – his final two kills were downed flying *Impossible Ince* (*Ince via Krane*)

For the next few weeks the weather provided the main opposition, with only one unescorted bombing raid (on 18 October) managing to penetrate a series of tropical storms that plagued the New Britain area. Coinciding with an improvement in the weather later in the month, the Fifth Air Force's P-38 groups commenced what would be one of their most successful periods in the Pacific with an escorted raid of Thirteenth Air Force bomber assets on 23 October. All fighter cover was provided by the Fifth until well into November when P-38s of the Thirteenth also began to escort bombers on missions to Rabaul – US Navy, Marine Corps and RNZAF attack units also benefited from Lightning fighter cover during this operation.

After days of cloud and rain, 23 October enjoyed a promising dawn, with just 6/10ths cloud cover on the way to the target, and diminishing scattered cumulus on the way home. No less than 47 P-38s covered the B-24s as they bombed Rapopo airfield, the fighters encountering a large force of Japanese interceptors stung into action after days of inactivity. The first to engage as the bombers approached the target was the 39th FS.

Nine-kill ace Paul Stanch had struggled to keep up with his squadronmates as they approached the target thanks to a rough-running engine in his P-38H-1 (42-66527), and as soon as the 39th engaged the enemy, he found himself surrounded by what he later identified as 'Oscars'. As he changed course and opened the throttles in an attempt to draw his six assailants away from the bomber stream, the offending engine began to stream coolant and overheat. Realising that this tactic was useless thanks to his precarious mechanical state, Stanch instead turned into a head-on attack with one of the enemy fighters. As the two machines closed at a combined speed of well over 600 mph, the American pilot saw many of his bullets and cannon shells explode into the Ki-43 from canopy to tail, before the 'Oscar' (or Zero) rolled beneath him and headed for the sea. One of the B-24 gunners, SSgt John Price, saw the aircraft hit the water, thus confirming Stanch's tenth, and last, victory.

As a footnote to the successful frontline tour of Paul Stanch, in the decades since the war many of his 39th FS comrades have tried to encourage him to attend squadron reunions, but the P-38 double ace has remained apart from social gatherings that have had anything to do with commemorating the conflict. Like many of the dutiful P-38 veterans of the period, Stanch performed this necessary, but unpleasant, task to the best of his ability, and then chose to turn his back on his wartime service.

Aside from Stanch's last combat victory, a number of other P-38 aces enjoyed success on the 23 October raid including Danny Roberts (P-38H-5 42-66752/'White 197'), who registered his eighth and ninth P-38 victories (two Zekes), and Jerry Johnson, who also bagged a Zeke for his seventh kill for the 9th FS. Future 431st aces Lts Marion Kirby (P-38H-1 42-66550) and Lowell Lutton (P-38H-5 42-66746) each downed Zeros (a 'Hamp' for the former and a Zeke for the latter), whilst Tom McGuire's regular wingman, Vincent Elliott (P-38H-1 42-66666), actually became the latest Lightning ace in-theatre when he claimed a Zeke and a 'Hamp'.

He had just pipped fellow 'Satan's Angel' Lt John Smith (P-38H-1 42-66539) of the 433rd FS in the race to make ace, the latter joining up with Elliott just in time to witness one of his victims plunging head-long into the depths off Rabaul. Not to be outdone, Smith, who had earlier become separated from his own flight, quickly accounted for his fifth victory when he shot down an 'Oscar' – Elliott got his second kill soon after. Once back at base, the authorities deemed it necessary to have Vincent Elliott swear under oath that he had indeed seen Smith destroy his opponent, since all other Lightning pilots in the vicinity had been too busy to notice the 'Oscar' crash.

On 24 October the assault on New Britain switched from high- to low-level bombing, USAAF B-25s attacking at wave-top height in what would soon become the most effective type of raid on the Rabaul installations. These missions would also prove to be both hazardous and rewarding for the P-38 units protecting the medium bombers – the Lightning's main opponents were the 201st and 204th Kokutais, the latter led by 11-kill ace Lt(jg) Sumio Fukuda.

No fewer than five P-38 pilots achieved their fifth confirmed victories on this date, with several other aces also adding to their scores over Rabaul. Lt Jay 'Cock' Robbins (P-38H-5 42-66820) was well on his way to becoming not only the top ace of the 80th FS but also the entire 8th FG when he claimed four 'Hamps' on the 24th, taking his score to 11 – he had also scored a quartet of Zeke kills the previous month (4 September, whilst flying the same Lightning) near Lae. Just prior to Robbins' cutting a swathe through the formation of 'Hamps', Frank Lent had downed his seventh victory (a 'Tony') directly over Rabaul whilst flying his favourite Lightning, P-38H-1 42-66550.

Also flying over New Britain on that late-morning sortie was Lt John G 'Jump' O'Neill who, as the leader of Green Flight of the 9th FS, was looking for his fifth kill to secure 'acedom'. As his formation approached the target area, O'Neill led them up to 6000 ft in order to better spot any intercepting Japanese fighters. Soon after they had levelled off a trio of Zekes were observed some 3000 ft below, so all four pilots in the flight jettisoned their belly tanks simultaneously and dove into the enemy. O'Neill made several ineffective passes until at last he fired a 45° burst from the rear and shot the entire tail section off one of the Mitsubishi fighters. Minutes later he got off a second telling burst that resulted in another Zeke flying directly into the side of a hill.

Lt Zach Dean (P-38H-1 42-66504) of the 432nd FS also claimed two

An anonymous groundcrewman from the 431st FS poses in front of the then Lt Tom McGuire's second Lightning (P-38H-5 42-66817/'White' 131, nicknamed *PUDGY*) whilst performing an engine change in early September 1943. It is likely that the 475th FG's leading ace scored at least five kills in this machine between late September and Boxing Day 1943

kills (a Zeke and a 'Hamp') to make him an ace on this date, whilst Lt Calvin Wire (P-38H-5 42-66753) of the 433rd FS repeated the same feat by destroying a pair of Zekes. Dean's squadron-mate, Lt Billy Gresham (P-38H-1 42-66568), went into the action on the 24th needing just a solitary Zeke to make ace, and this he duly claimed during the course of the morning.

Lt Cornelius 'Corky' Smith (P-38H-1 42-66668) of the 80th FS managed to find himself embroiled in a long-running combat with a number of black-painted 'Hamps' whose pilots impressed Smith with their dogfighting skills. Due to the agility of his opponents, Smith was only given the fleeting opportunity to face each enemy fighter in turn head-on. Such was the nature of this twisting engagement, Smith and his wingman, Lt Paul 'Blue Eyes' Murphey (P-38F-5 42-12643), flashed past each of their assailants on several occasions. After what seemed like hours of ceaseless high-g manoeuvring, Murphey managed to score a direct hit on one of the 'Hamps', which exploded in front of him (this was his second kill, and he would finish his tour in April 1945 with six victories). He then informed his leader that he was 'low on gas'.

Breaking off the dogfight, Smith and Murphey sighted a damaged 39th FS P-38 nearby and escorted it out of the area. During the return trip to Port Moresby, the former had to feather an engine due to the paucity of his fuel supply – a reflection of the full throttle nature of the long-running dogfight over Rabaul. During debriefing Smith learned that one of the 'Hamps' he had attacked was seen to crash, so he was now a P-38 ace! The 80th FS had performed particularly well on this day, gaining a record 12 victories during its many patrols over Rabaul.

Allied bombers returned to high altitude sorties on the 25th, but once

**Lt Frank Lent was a high-spirited ace from Minneapolis, Minnesota, who scored steadily from the moment the 475th FG commenced operations in August 1943. He claimed a trio of victories over Oro Bay on 15 October 1943 to take his score to five, and then got two more over Rabaul several weeks later. Lent's final two kills (which took his score up to 11) comprised a pair of Zekes downed south of Hollandia on 31 March 1944. Capt F J Lent was killed in a flying accident off Lae on 1 December 1944 when his F-6D Mustang hit the sea whilst on an impromptu test flight (*Dennis Cooper*)**

again the weather interfered with the operation and most B-24 and B-25s had to turn back, along with their P-38 escorts. Future 475th FG CO Maj Charles H MacDonald left his office at Dobodura HQ on this day to fly at the head of the 432nd FS, charging newly-crowned ace Zach Dean with the responsibility of watching his back. Despite the adverse weather, the major was determined to offer protection for those bombers that pressed on with the mission.

He took his small force of fighters up to 27,500 ft in and effort to fly over the worst of weather, and emerged on the other side of the front as the only real fighter deterrent between the Japanese interceptors and the vulnerable bombers. Realising that for once the Liberators were not protected by large numbers of Lightnings, the enemy pilots did not take long to press home their attacks, and MacDonald's earphones were soon full of cries for help from the beleaguered B-24 crews. The handful of P-38 pilots in the immediate vicinity of Rabaul were kept busy darting in and out of the bomber formation repelling Japanese fighters. Despite having to rapidly move from one B-24 to the next, shooting fighters off their tails as he went, MacDonald did manage to hit a single Zeke with a prolonged burst over Vunakanau Field, sending it down in flames. It was the only claim for the mission on either side, and Japanese records seem to verify the victory by stating that one Mitsubishi fighter failed to return. With confirmation of his kill coming from another P-38 pilot, 'Mac' MacDonald had secured his fourth victory – he would go on to score 23 more.

The weather failed to improve over the next three days, forcing the complete cancellation of scheduled missions to Rabaul until 29 October, when another high altitude mission was flown. If this raid had been a low-level strike, the damage inflicted on the enemy's bases would perhaps have been more severe, and provoked a greater response from the hard-pressed sentais who were struggling to make good pilot losses suffered just a week earlier. As it was, the B-24s encountered something less than a totally committed Japanese fighter force, although the P-38s still claimed some 18 Zeros destroyed for the loss of a single 432nd FS pilot and his aircraft.

Two more P-38 pilots became aces on this mission. The first of these was 'Charlie' King (P-38H-5 42-66822), who had been recently promoted to major and put in charge of the 39th FS. He scored his first victories as CO of the unit when he downed a Zeke and an 'Oscar' near Vunakanau airfield.

P-38J-5 42-67147/'White 168' wears both distinctive nose-art and the associated nickname *Black Market Babe*. This particular machine was the mount of 432nd FS six-kill ace Lt Billy Gresham, who probably downed his final victory in '*Babe* on 18 January 1944 – he also claimed a probable kill in a J-5 on 31 March. Like Frank Lent, Gresham was killed in a flying accident, his parachute streaming when he bailed out of a new P-38L north of Biak on 2 October 1944

**Lt Perry Dahl poses by the nose of his P-38H-1 *SKIDOO*" (42-66504/ 'White 162') at Dobodura in late 1943. This aeroplane was 'Pee Wee' Dahl's first mount within the 432nd FS, and he immediately put it to good use by scoring his premier victory – an 'Oscar', downed over Alexishafen – on his combat debut on 9 November 1943. Dahl finished the war with nine kills (all scored with the 432nd FS), and later went on to complete two frontline flying tours in Viet Nam with the 56th Special Operations Wing almost three decades later**

These were his fourth and fifth victories, and they were recorded in glorious colour as King had had a roll of experimental film loaded in his gun camera to check the advantages of colour over black and white in separating the various shades of sea, sky and jungle in post-sortie debriefs.

The second ace of the day was the 9th FS's Lt Ralph Wandrey, who had had several bad experiences during various flights to Rabaul, including nearly colliding with other friendly aircraft in a wild mix-up while flying on instruments through cloud. On the 29th, however, he caught a Zeke at altitude in the clear whilst flying an old P-38F-2 and despatched it to claim his fifth victory. Wandrey got a further kill in March of the following year after his unit's forced re-equipment with P-47s, and by the time he returned to the US in August 1944, he had flown 191 missions.

By the end of October Allied planners in New Guinea were confident that the back of Japanese resistance in the Rabaul area had been broken. In reality, Japanese morale had been shaken by the raids but was nonetheless intact, and reinforcements had been flown in to bolster the air defence during the extended period of bad weather. Thus, the Americans confidently scheduled another low-level bomber mission for 2 November, thinking that their P-38 escorts would be opposed by little more than the remnants of the Japanese fighter force. However, once over the target the Lightning and Mitchell squadrons encountered the stiffest aerial opposition of the entire Rabaul campaign in a mission that would subsequently be dubbed 'Bloody Tuesday' by its survivors.

The Allied plan of action was for elements of the 39th and 80th FSs to sweep in ahead of the main bomber formation and clear away any Japanese fighter presence in their path, while the 9th FS and the squadrons of the 475th FG would cover the B-25s over the target. The plan began to unravel right at the beginning of the mission, however, as the first flights of P-38s became separated by a cloud layer, resulting in elements of the 39th FS meeting little opposition at all above the clouds, whilst at the same time the 80th FS was forced to fight for its life against a veritable 'hornet's nest' of Japanese fighters below the overcast.

The latter unit finally withdrew due to shortage of fuel, rather than opponents, after a vicious fight that had brought its pilots nine new victories for the loss of two P-38s. During the chaotic dogfight at low-level, Lt Allen Hill (P-38G-15 43-2211) had downed two Zekes and claimed a third as a probable, all of which doubled his previous score. Fellow 80th FS pilots Lts Ed 'Indian Joe' DeGraffenreid (six kills in total – P-38F-5 42-12643) and John Jones (eight kills in total – P-38H-5 42-66820), meanwhile, had claimed their last confirmed victories of the war, each being credited with one Zero and a probable.

The 80th's Lt Louis Schriber (P-38G-15 43-2299) had undoubtedly endured the most frustrating day on this occasion, for having fought until his fuel ran low, he was forced to return to base with no evidence to support his claims of four Zeros shot down, having instead to settle for probable kills – aside from his final tally of five confirmed victories, 'Screwy Louie' Schriber would finish the war with six probable kills.

Despite having heard frantic radio calls for assistance from the outnumbered 80th FS pilots up ahead, Capt Jerry 'Johnnie Eager' Johnson lived up to his nickname as he led Red Flight of the 9th FS into battle from the north-east at a height of 3000 ft – the survivors of the 39th and

80th FSs used the arrival of the close-escort Lightning units as their opportunity to break off the engagement and retire safely homeward.

Johnson quickly spotted a small formation of enemy fighters climbing out from Lakunai airfield and wasted no time in ordering external fuel tanks to be jettisoned in preparation for combat. Thanks to his height and speed advantage, he soon had his P-38 perfectly positioned for a textbook 45° gunnery pass on a 'Zeke' that was struggling to gain altitude with its own drop tank still firmly attached. The 9th FS pilot opened fire and his foe immediately began to shed pieces of fuselage before crashing not too far from Lakunai.

With one kill already under his belt and dozens of enemy aircraft still milling around over Rabaul, Johnson's hunting instincts came to the fore and he quickly centred an 'Oscar' in his sights. However, despite firing a number of rounds at the JAAF fighter, the Ki-43 managed to escape unscathed, but a second Zeke encountered moments later was not so lucky. Although the downing of Johnson's second kill had caused his own guns to start to burn out, he nevertheless made attacks on at least six other Zeros and 'Oscars', before chasing an enemy fighter off the tail of another P-38. By now low on fuel, and with most of his guns inoperable, 'Johnnie Eager' decided that it was time to return to base.

Like the 80th FS, the 431st endured a rough time over Rabaul on the 2nd protecting the bombers under its care, although Marion Kirby (P-38H-5 42-66827) made the most of the many opportunities presented to the unit to engage the enemy by shooting down two Zekes to become a Lightning ace. One of his victims was almost certainly Japanese ace Yoshi-o Fukui of the *Zuiho* Fighter Squadron, who would end the war with 11 victories. The latter had just shot down a B-25 at low-level when his Zeke was hit by fire from a P-38 (Japanese records indicate that Fukai was 'sur-

The legendary Capt Danny Roberts poses for an official USAAF photographer at Dobodura in his mount (P-38H-5 42-66752/'White 197') in late October 1943. CO of the 433rd FS, Roberts used this Lightning to down five Zekes in a week between 17 and 24 October 1943. His 14th, and last, victory was against a 'Hamp' over Alexishafen on the morning of 9 November 1943, Roberts losing his life just minutes later when he collided with his wingman whilst attempting to manoeuvre in behind a second Japanese fighter
(*Dennis Glen Cooper*)

rounded' by a formation of Lightnings) and was forced to take to his parachute. Despite Fukui having claimed to have been overwhelmed by a number of P-38s, postwar analysis of Kirby's combat report shows that he was the only pilot to claim a Zero destroyed just after it had downed a B-25.

Three P-38 pilots became aces during this frenetic mission, including two from the same formation. The 431st FS's 'Hades White Flight' was being led on this occasion by seasoned ex-9th FS P-40E pilot Lt Art Wenige (P-38H-1 42-66511), who had scored three kills up to this point in his tour (one in P-40E 41-5648 and two in an earlier mission in P-38H-1 42-66511). He made ace in style during this sortie, claiming two Zekes destroyed near Rabaul – Wenige claimed his final kill of the war five days later when he downed a 'Tony' near Adler Bay again in '511.

Fellow 'Hades White Flight' member Lowell Lutton (P-38H-5 42-66821) was the second 431st FS pilot to get his fifth kill on the 2nd, shooting a Zeke off the tail of another P-38. He had little time to enjoy his new ace status, however, as he was either wounded in the fight or ran out of gas on the way home, for he simply disappeared out of sight of the other flight members on the return leg to Dobodura and was subsequently listed as Missing In Action.

The third pilot to make ace on this mission was Lt Grover 'Goon' Gholson, who had been in-theatre since early 1942 flying P-39Fs with the 36th FS. He had scored his first kill – a Zero – as early as 14 May 1942, although he was shot down in an Airacobra and slightly wounded just 15 days later. Due to his extensive frontline experience, Gholson was amongst the select band of pilots picked from the 8th FG to staff the newly-formed 432nd FS of the 475th FG in May 1943, and had gone on to claim two more victories up to 2 November. During the infamous 'Bloody Tuesday' mission whilst flying P-38H-5 42-66832, he was involved in a running fight that netted him both an 'Oscar' and a Zeke for his fourth and fifth victories. These were Gholson's final kills.

Seven days later a smaller raid was sent out to test the defences of Rabaul so that 'Bloody Tuesday' would not be repeated, and during the course of the mission two pilots scored sufficient kills to make them the final Fifth Air Force P-38 aces of the campaign. Lt Jack Mankin (P-38H-1 42-66537) of the 431st FS destroyed a 'Tony' and an 'Oscar' to take his score to exactly five, whilst Lt Allen Hill (P-38H-5 42-66820) added a Zeke to his quartet of previous victories over the ubiquitous Mitsubishi fighter to also achieve 'acedom'. The latter would go on to score a further four kills (ironically, none of which were Zekes) in 1944 flying P-38J/Ls, but Mankin remained on five kills to war's end.

Aircraft from both the Thirteenth Air Force and the US Navy would

**Capt Joe McKeon was amongst the handful of pilots transferred from the 8th to the 475th FG. He had already scored a single victory in a P-39D-1 (41-38353) with the 35th FS, and went on to claim a further four kills (including two in this very Lightning) in P-38s. McKeon's final victory was scored on the other side of the globe when he downed a Luftwaffe Bf 109G over Germany whilst flying a P-51D with the 77th FS/20th FG on 16 August 1944 (*McKeon*)**

**Nicknamed 'Johnnie Eager', Jerry Johnson earned this sobriquet by the way he 'waded' into Japanese formations with utter fearlessness whilst leading the 9th FS (*USAF*)**

join the Fifth Air Force in a massive raid on 11 November to signal both the end of Fifth Fighter Command's campaign in the Pacific and the beginning of Thirteenth Fighter Command's operations against Rabaul. Between December 1943 and the end of February 1944, P-38s of the Thirteenth Air Force would clash with ever-diminishing numbers of Japanese aircraft around Rabaul until the latter were withdrawn completely in order to face the advancing Allied forces in the Central Pacific area.

Maj Bob Westbrook, CO of the 44th FS/18th FG, and ranking ace of the group by war's end, earned the Distinguished Service Cross for a series of volunteer sweeps to the Rabaul area in December 1943. During the sorties flown between the 23rd and 25th of this month, he claimed five victories and two shared (all Zekes) in his P-38H/J, plus claimed another Mitsubishi fighter as damaged. Westbrook had been with the 44th – known as the 'Vampires' – since August 1942, and had scored his first kill on 27 January 1943 over Guadalcanal in a P-40F.

By the time his unit received P-38s in the early autumn of 1943, Westbrook's score had risen to seven, and he went on to achieve his first Lightning victories on 10 October whilst flying as wingman to Bill Harris (of 339th FS fame) on a B-24 escort to Kahili – although now a major, and CO of the 44th FS, Westbrook realised that it would be wise to gain experience on his new type before leading his unit into action, hence his decision to fly as wingman to veteran P-38 ace Harris, who was only a first lieutenant. A number of Zeros intercepted the bombers and soon shot one down, but Harris exacted swift retribution by destroying three enemy fighters in short order. 'Westy' Westbrook's previous experience in the P-40 stood him in good stead too, and he claimed another Zero, plus shared a probable with his flight lead. Six other Zeros were claimed by the rest of the formation, including two for Jim Shubin.

Westbrook then had to wait until the trio of B-24 escort missions flown in the lead up to Christmas Day 1943 before he was presented with the chance to register his next victories. On the first of these sorties no less than 28 Japanese interceptors were claimed to havé been destroyed by US Navy/USMC Corsair pilots, whilst two other Zekes were downed by Westbrook and a third by another pilot in his flight. The following day brought a trio of Zeke victories as the major led his unit in a sweep ahead of the bombers, thus making Westbrook a P-38 ace. Christmas Day saw another raid on Rabaul's Lakunai airfield, and the 44th FS claimed four Zeros for the loss of two P-38s – half of the kills fell to Westbrook, taking his score to 14 victories.

On 6 January the 44th ran into another fight with 30 Zekes over the Rabaul area, and by the time the P-38s broke off the combat through a shortage of fuel, the unit had shot down nine Zeros for the loss of two

Lt John 'Jump' O'Neill finally achieved ace status with the 9th FS during the fierce fighting over Rabaul in the last two weeks of October 1943, scoring six kills in exactly 14 days – he had previously downed two Japanese fighters some seven months before

Having been forced to feather an engine due to a lack of fuel, Lt Cornelius 'Corky' Smith gingerly brings P-38H-1 42-66668/'Yellow S' – nicknamed *CORKY Jr* – in to land at Port Moresby on 24 October 1943 after an eventful sortie over Kabanga Bay, off Rabaul. Smith had 'made ace' during this sortie, although at the time this shot was taken he was unaware that one of the Zekes he had tangled with had indeed crashed (*Smith*)

The 80th FS's Lt 'Screwy' Louis Schriber was in the thick of the fighting during the 'Bloody Tuesday' action of 2 November 1943, claiming two Zeros and two Zekes over Rabaul. Unfortunately, all four claims went down as probables, and he would have to wait until late 1944 before achieving ace status

Lightnings – Westbrook got one kill. The exquisitely named Capt Cotesworth Bradway Head, Jr, of the 44th FS also claimed one of the Zekes downed on this mission (plus a 'Hamp' probable), marking his first success in a P-38. He went on to destroy a further five aircraft over the next 12 days to become the 44th FS's second Lightning ace. Head's victories included a B5N 'Kate' torpedo bomber on the 14th, a trio of Zekes off Rabaul on the 17th and a final Mitsubishi fighter off New Britain 24 hours later – he was killed soon after scoring this final victory when shot down by another Zeke whilst flying P-38J-5 42-67155. Aside from Head's tally of six kills in the Lightning, he had earlier claimed eight victories whilst flying P-40F/M Warhawks, again with the 44th FS.

The 339th FS/347th FG celebrated their return to action over Rabaul on 24 January 1944 by claiming four Zekes, all of which fell to future aces of the unit. Lt Truman Barnes got two, while Capt George Chandler and Lt Thomas Walker each claimed single kills. Chandler, who had earlier claimed a trio of victories in the Solomons in 1943, became a Lightning ace when he claimed another Zeke over Rabaul on 3 February.

Like Chandler, Tom Walker had also tasted success with the 339th during the push up from Guadalcanal in 1943 by claiming three kills, and finally 'made ace' exactly a week after his squadron-mate when he destroyed a Zeke – Truman Barnes got his third 'scalp' on the dame day. Henry Meigs of nightfighting fame over Guadalcanal got his fifth and sixth victories over Rabaul on 15 February, while Truman Barnes became the last ace of the Thirteenth Air Force when he claimed two more Zeros over Rabaul three days later.

From March 1944 until VJ-Day, Rabaul's threat to the Allied plan of action in the Pacific gradually receded to the point where it became a virtual backwater of the war. Bombing raids continued for a time, but no significant actions were directed either from or toward the base. Fifth and Thirteenth Air Force P-38s had played a major part in battering the once mighty air forces stationed there into oblivion.

## HOLLANDIA

After neutralising Rabaul, the Allies were able to swiftly advance into the Central and South-west Pacific. The Gilbert, Marshall and Admiralties Islands fell into their hands during February-March 1944, thus breaching the outer ring of the Imperial defences in the process.

On New Guinea the situation was decidedly desperate for the Japanese. The only base through which supplies and reinforcements could be channelled to Japanese forces in the region was the old Dutch colonial city of Hollandia, which was now well within escort range of the P-38. Hollandia was scheduled to be invaded by the end of April 1944, following the usual campaign of aerial bombardment – between 30 March and 12 April five raids were flown against the base, netting P-38 pilots roughly 60 victories, and offering the aces their last opportunity to score heavily against the Japanese over New Guinea.

The sheer effort expended by the USAAF's fighter units in the raids on New Britain had cost them dearly in terms of destroyed, damaged or just simply worn out P-38s. Indeed, so bad was the situation that the 9th and 39th FSs were forced to relinquish their Lightnings in favour of the more plentiful P-47D Thunderbolt, and only the former unit would return to the P-38 after operations over Hollandia were completed. The chronic shortage of Lightning fighters in-theatre was due to the fact that USAAF air forces in Europe had priority in the receipt of new aircraft, and their demand easily absorbed Lockheed's production output.

If the USAAF felt that the numerical strength of their escort force would barely cover the bombers tasked with attacking Hollandia (the 80th and the three units of the 475th FG were the only P-38 assets available), then the situation facing the Japanese was dire in the extreme. Only four fighter sentai could be raised to protect Hollandia from its Allied attackers – the 33rd, 77th and 248th equipped with 'Oscars' and the 68th with 'Tonys'.

These units were staffed by relatively inexperienced crews who had recently been flown out from flying schools in Japan as attrition replacements, whilst their opponents – although equally small in number – were mostly seasoned veterans of the Wewak and Rabaul operations. Experience was not their only advantage, however, for the American pilots also enjoyed the irresistible momentum generated by past victories in New Guinea and the Solomons. In addition, the priorities of the European theatre were finally beginning to abate with the arrival of the definitive P-51B/C Mustang in England and Italy. The immediate effect of this was felt with the delivery of 58 factory-fresh P-38Js to New Guinea at the end of February.

The first raid on 30 March comprised about 80 B-24s escorted by every available P-38 from both the 80th FS and the 475th FG. Again the Americans seemed to have achieved total surprise over the target for the Japanese response was weak and ineffective. The only engagement recorded saw a number of 80th FS flights claim seven 'Oscars' and 'Tonys' destroyed for no loss.

Leading one of the 'Headhunter' flights was now Capt Jay 'Cock' Robbins, who had not seen combat since recording his 13th kill over Cape Gloucester on Boxing Day 1943. Flying into a random formation of 'Oscars' after he had reported their position to other elements of the 475th, he ordered his

Lt Ken Ladd (left) had scored eight kills by the time this shot was taken with his crewchief at Nadzab in late February 1944. He went on to claim a further two kills over Hollandia in late March/early April, later stating that the pilots encountered over the enemy base during these combats seemed to be lacking in aggression, thus presenting easy prey for marauding P-38s. Ladd's final tally totalled 12 victories, his last two kills being scored just prior to his death on 14 October 1944 over Balikpapan, Borneo, during combat with a large force of 'Oscar IIs'

Maj John Loisel (smoking a cigarette) played a major part in shaping the impressive record achieved by the 475th FG in combat, firstly while in command of the 432nd FS, and later the entire group. This shot shows Loisel and his groundcrew at Dobodura during early 1944, the former's P-38H-1 (42-66682/'White 161'), nicknamed *SCREAMIN' KID*, serving as a backdrop – Loisel downed at least two (possibly four) Zekes in this fighter. The pilot standing at the far left in this photograph is fellow 432nd FS ace Billy Gresham (*Loisel*)

flight to drop their external tanks and select targets at will. Driving on through light flak thrown up by Japanese AA batteries on the ground, Robbins managed to damage one 'Oscar' before registering a confirmed kill against a second Ki-43, which exploded in front of him. This initial attack dispersed the remaining Japanese fighters who were vainly trying to get through to the bombers. Robbins then climbed up into another formation of 'Oscars' that was hell-bent on tackling the Liberators and fought a Ki-43 down to tree top level, where it crashed into the side of a hill.

Rabaul veteran Lt Louis Schriber followed Robbins through his wild gyrations and watched both 'Oscars' crash. He then got behind a 'Tony' and managed to stay with the fighter through a straining 'split-s' manoeuvre before he finally shot it down in flames – this was his second confirmed kill of 1944, having been frustrated over New Britain in 1943 when he had been forced to lodge claims for five probables and not a single victory! Before he turned for home, Schriber noticed that the Japanese interceptors seemed disorganised in their attacks and not very aggressive, particularly in comparison to the defenders of Rabaul, and that the anti-aircraft fire was generally inaccurate.

Seasoned 80th FS ace Ken Ladd also sensed the lack of fighting spirit in his opponents when he led his own flight down to attack a retreating Japanese force that only offered him enough resistance to get one of their number damaged and another probably destroyed. Ladd had a reputation for aggressive airmanship when engaged in combat, and he achieved most of his 12 victories through the dogged pursuit of his enemy, but even a spirited chase over a number of minutes with his P-38J-15 screaming at full throttle failed to overhaul the determined retreat of the Ki-61s. The 'Tony' that he claimed as probably destroyed was actually shared with his old buddy 'Cy' Homer, who generously tried to give Ladd confirmation for the Japanese fighter in his combat report. The latter did managed to help confirm another 'Tony' for Homer, however, as he witnessed a fighter attacked by him crash into the water off Hollandia prior to giving chase to his Ki-61 – this was Homer's ninth kill.

The next day another force of B-24s, again covered by P-38s, struck Hollandia, but this time the Japanese responded with a more co-ordinated fighter defence that offered more opportunities of combat to the USAAF pilots. This time both the 80th and 431st FSs engaged the interceptors, claiming 14 aircraft destroyed for the loss of a single P-38.

'Screwy' Louis Schriber got his third confirmed victory during this sortie when he followed Jay Robbins into an attack on an 'Oscar'. The former anticipated the Ki-43 pilot performing a 'split-s' and duly dropped below the fight by about 1500 ft. He was quickly proved right as the 'Oscar' dropped out of Robbins' gunsight and promptly turned directly into Schriber's! The fighter was shot down with a burst that raked the fuselage from 'stem to stern'.

Denied on this occasion, 'Cock' Robbins soon slotted in behind another 'Oscar' and clinically despatched his quarry before it had time to manoeuvre away, thus notching up his 16th victory. Having been frustrated by the negative tactics of the Japanese 24 hours earlier, Ken Ladd made certain of his prey on this mission by getting so close to it that the oil from the dying 'Oscar' sprayed all over Ladd's windscreen. Now Capt 'Corky' Smith encountered an unusual target over Hollandia in the form of a Ki-46 'Dinah' reconnaissance aircraft that had wandered into the battle area whilst trying to return to its base following the completion of a photographic sortie. Although quick, the Mitsubishi 'twin' was no match for a P-38J-15, and after a long and involved pursuit at varying heights Smith finally shot it down.

The 431st FS accounted for exactly half of the victories scored on 31 March, with its second ranking ace Lt Frank Lent downing two 'Oscars' to take his score to 11 (his final tally) and future ace Lt Frank Monk claiming another Ki-43 – although he reported it as a Zeke – for his fourth kill.

3 April 1944 was the most successful day for the Hollandia escort fighters, who claimed no less than 25 enemy interceptors for the loss of just a solitary P-38. Ken Ladd again got a single 'Oscar' kill (his tenth), commenting at his debrief back at base that the Japanese seemed a little bit more determined than on their previous two visits to the Hollandia area.

This mission was carried out by a combined force of B-24s at high altitude, covered by the 80th FS, followed by B-25s and A-20s who had the entire 475th FG 'riding shotgun' for them. These low-flying 'bombing

Dick Bong, Tom Lynch and the former's P-38J-15 (42-103993, nicknamed *Marge*) are captured in an informal pose at Cape Gloucester in mid-March 1944. Bong scored four victories in this machine, which was one of the first natural metal Lightnings to see action in the Pacific. It was lost just days after this shot was taken on 24 March when it crashed whilst on a weather-check sortie over the New Guinea coast, the aircraft's pilot, Lt Tom Malone, managing to abandon the fighter and make his way back to safety. A close examination of this shot reveals that *Marge*'s scoreboard is mysteriously adorned with 25 victory flags – Bong didn't score his 25th confirmed kill until 3 April 1944 whilst on a mission to Hollandia!

twins' would drop 'parafrags' (fragmentation bombs dropped at the ends of parachutes) and strafe whatever undamaged aircraft or installations existed following the Liberators' strike. By the end of this complex mission the threat posed by the surviving Japanese force in Hollandia would be negligible.

Leading 'Copper Blue Flight', 'Cy' Homer had his best day of the war whilst protecting the B-24s under his charge – he claimed two 'Tonys' and two 'Oscars' that attempted to break through the escorting fighters to attack the vulnerable Liberators. The two Ki-61s were hit so quickly with accurate bursts from Homer's P-38J-15 that they both crashed in flames within sight of each other.

Lt 'C B' Ray was flying on 'Corky' Smith's wing when a group of 'Oscars' attempted to engage the B-24s just as they were leaving the target. The Japanese attackers were so intent on downing the bombers that they failed to see Ray slip in directly behind them – the trailing Ki-43 was hit in the wingroot by a well-aimed burst and the fighter spiralled down in flames.

The 475th FG was led into action on this day by none other than now Lt Col Charles MacDonald, who had been in charge of the group since November of the previous year. Flying his personal P-38J-15 42-104024/'Blue 100' *PUTT-PUTT MARU*, 'Mac' had chosen to head up the 432nd FS, who had been briefed to cover the A-20s at the end of their attack run – often the point at which the bombers were at their most spread out, and therefore vulnerable, and also when the Japanese fighters were mostly likely to strike.

Seasoned ace Capt John Loisel was leading the 432nd's 'Clover Blue Flight' on this occasion, and his team was the first to respond when a number of A-20 crews spotted enemy fighters diving in to attack. Loisel quickly placed his flight between the bombers and the intercepting fighters and proceeded to engage the enemy over Hollandia's Lake Sentani. Two of the attacking 'Oscars' crashed into the hills around the lake, giving Loisel victories number nine and ten – in the heat of battle the captain had mistakenly identified one of the Ki-43 as a 'Hamp'. His element leader, Lt Perry 'Pee Wee' Dahl, also got a pair of 'Oscars' (he too claimed one as a Zeke), registering his fourth and fifth victories in the process.

The best show of the day, however, was put up by the 432nd FS's Lt Joe Forster, who was filling the somewhat vulnerable 'Tailend-Charlie' position within 'Clover Blue Flight'. Forster had arrived in the 432nd at the same time as Dahl, but had only registered two Zeke probables in combat until this mission, when he finally 'broke his duck' by claiming two 'Tonys' and an 'Oscar'.

Whilst in the process of manoeuvring in behind the formation of Ki-43s, Forster noticed that a new and unpainted P-38J had slipped in on his wing, and it quickly proceeded to shoot down one of the 'Oscars' near the western shoreline of Sentani Lake. The 432nd pilot was feeling rather indignant at the sheer cheek of the uninvited upstart who had 'crashed his party' until he received a request over the radio for confirmation of the kill from none other now Maj Richard Bong of Fifth Fighter Command – Forster had just witnessed the destruction of the latter's 25th victory.

The last Hollandia mission on which Japanese aircraft would be claimed was flown on 12 April. Jay Robbins claimed two 'Tonys' during

Arguably one of America's greatest ever aviators, the truly legendary Charles Lindbergh extensively toured the Pacific theatre in 1944, flying a number of missions with various frontline P-38 units, including the 8th and 475th FGs. Indeed, he even managed to shoot down a Japanese aircraft whilst on a patrol with the latter group in the summer of 1944 – an action which resulted in 475th boss Col Charles 'Mac' MacDonald being recalled to the US for three months on disciplinary grounds! Lindbergh is seen here at around that time with 431st CO Maj Tom McGuire, the latter astonishing other senior officers within the 475th FG with his unseemly taunting of the famed transatlantic pilot during his stay with the group at Biak. Lindbergh, however, took the barbs with good grace, and reportedly set McGuire on his heels a time or two himself the course of the sortie – one over the shore line of Sentani Lake and the other just off the Hollandia strip whilst bombs from attacking B-24s at high altitude were falling all around him! 'Corky' Smith got his 11th, and last, victory in the same area, whilst Capt Burnell Adams, (an ex-P-70 nightfighter pilot who had pleaded and wangled his way into combat with the 80th after scoring a solitary claim with the 6th NFS in May 1943), downed a 'Tony' and an 'Oscar' for his fourth and fifth P-38 kills.

Adams observed something else of even greater historical significance than his own achievement of making ace on this mission. A natural-metal P-38J-15LO (42-104012) boasting red trim had joined up with the 80th FS soon after take-off and hitched a ride into the combat zone with the unit. Once engaged with the enemy, Adams, and his wingman Lt Nick Zinni, had observed the unpainted P-38 shoot down at least a pair of 'Oscars' (they missed a third Ki-43 that was later credited to the anonymous Lightning) which would give its pilot, Maj Richard Ira Bong, 27 confirmed victories. He thus became the first officially recognised American fighter pilot to surpass Capt Eddie Rickenbacker's mythical World War 1 record of 26 aeroplanes and balloons shot down.

By the time Bong had secured his place in USAAF history, the bombing campaign against Hollandia had been all but completed. Only one more mission remained to be flown, and this took place on 16 April. Despite no Japanese fighters being met on this occasion, the outcome of the raid was disastrous for the Allied fighters and bombers that took part, as they encountered an enemy that even the P-38 could not overcome – the weather. Having dropped their ordnance unmolested, the bombers turned around and headed for home, but the appearance of a sudden tropical front blocked the way of the returning American aircraft and forced the entire group into a blinding mass of rain clouds. Dozens of aircraft were lost as they ran out of fuel, or simply hit the ground disorientated thanks to the treacherous New Guinea weather.

Despite this tragic end to the Hollandia campaign, the successes enjoyed by the Allies in their raids against the key Japanese bases in the region meant that the battle for New Guinea had, for all intents and purposes, been won. Only mopping up operations against embattled pockets of Japanese resistance (now totally devoid of air cover) had still to be completed, leaving Allied strategists to turn their attention towards the next great offensive – the recapturing of the Philippines.

Capt 'Corky' Smith stands by his P-38J, nicknamed *CORKY IV*, at Nadzab in May 1944, just weeks before his tour ended and he returned home. Smith downed 11 aircraft during the 169 missions he completed with the 80th FS, which were flown between November 1942 and May 1944 (*Smith via Rocker*)

# LESSONS FROM HOLLANDIA

Hollandia had fallen so quickly following the overwhelming Allied bombing campaign that many crated Japanese aircraft sent out to help defend the last bastion of the Imperial Empire in the South-west Pacific had been left on the receiving docks in their packing cases. The enemy had been so surprised by the swiftness of the assault on the ground in the aftermath of the bombing raids that there was simply no escape route planned for JAAF assets, forcing many pilots and groundcrews to make either an overland retreat to Sarmi along the coast, or to the Japanese stronghold at Babo, inland near the Vogelkop peninsula. Many of the retreating airmen fell victim to strafing by Allied aircraft along the way, whilst others simply succumbed to the rigors of the trek or were captured in hand-to-hand fighting with Australian and American troops on the ground. The sheer magnitude of the overwhelming defeat inflicted on the Japanese at Hollandia is reflected in the fact that none of the JAAF units that deployed to the area during the final weeks of its defence survived the battle to fight again – only a handful of airmen escaped on foot to eventually be reassigned to new sentai.

One of the many JAAF personnel captured in the aftermath of the fall of Hollandia was Lt Masao Oishihashi, an intelligence officer of the 77th Sentai who was picked up while foraging for food on 29 July 1944. His interrogation provided some interesting views on combat in the area, and his comments regarding the P-38 were typical of those gleaned from many Japanese prisoners of war. They are summarised here in Interrogation Report No 600;

'Japs had a great respect for the performance of this airplane, and were amazed at its formation attacks, quick climbing ability, and fine results achieved. Jap fighters could not cope with the formation attacks, particularly when P-38s operated line astern. Jap pilots in an 'Oscar' or 'Tony', felt they had a good chance against a P-38 in solo combat, but against a formation attack they had no chance.'

American experience confirmed this view of the P-38. The basic attack formation for both sides in the Pacific War seemed to be the 'string' formation, or line astern, with one fighter following another into the inter-

Maj Dick Bong's P-38J-15 as seen in late April 1944, soon after the Hollandia campaign. The concentrated firepower housed in the nose fairing of the P-38 was widely respected by German and Japanese pilots alike, the fighter's cannon fitment giving it a more lethal punch than other US fighters. This aircraft is probably 42-104012, which was used by Bong to score his 26th, 27th and 28th victories over Hollandia on 12 April 1944

Camera evidence of one of Bong's victories. The 'Oscar' is centered in the aperture of the camera at close range. Note the fighter's open canopy, suggesting that the pilot was either surprised or attempting to abandon his aircraft

Fifth Fighter Command's Maj Tom Lynch captured his kill over a Ki-48 'Lily' on film on the afternoon of 10 February 1944. The bomber was shot down over Tadji airstrip, New Guinea – four weeks later its victor was also to crash to his death in the same location, his Lightning having been hit by AA fire. As with Bong's kill shown on the opposing page, note that Lynch has his target centred in the camera frame at close range (*Charles King*)

This P-38G-5 is reckoned to be the Lightning used by the newly-promoted Capt Dick Bong to gain his 16th victory (an 'Oscar') 28 July 1943 north-west of Rein Bay. Note the rudimentary eye painted behind the spinner on the port engine. Seen here at the 9th FS's Dobodura base, 'White 73' was taken out of service and reduced to components soon after this photo was taken as a result of the battle damage it had suffered whilst being flown by Bong

ception. All P-38 units in Fifth Fighter Command stressed the importance in maintaining the flight, or at least elements of two fighters. Many of the P-38s that did not return from combat missions were flown by pilots who either could not, or would not, join up with other P-38 formations and were simply picked off by the more agile Japanese fighters, which 'hunted' in packs. The latter were especially adept at bouncing single P-38s, having often lured an individual out of a formation through the use of a seemingly vulnerable lone fighter at low altitude. Unbeknown to the Lightning pilot that gave chase to this 'sitting duck' as it tried to climb away, other Japanese veteran pilots would be laying in wait at higher altitudes.

Many of the P-38 aces preferred to meet Japanese fighters head on, Dick Bong especially showing a strong inclination to attack from this angle. The 'Oscar' was particularly vulnerable from the front, and its inferior armament of just two 12.7 mm machine-guns mounted above the engine cowling were no match for the P-38's overwhelming mix of machine-guns and cannon – Bong claimed at least 10 of the 21 victories in his first tour of duty with head-on attacks. One of the great advantages enjoyed by USAAF pilots employing this tactic was that it negated the superior manoeuvrability of the nimble Zero and 'Oscar'.

The head-on attack was less effective when engaging a 'Tony', however, as the Kawasaki fighter possessed a smaller frontal area thanks to its inline engine. It also boasted a substantially heavier armament than the 'Oscar', carrying either a quartet of machine-guns (7.7 and 12.7 mm weapons) or a mix of two 12.7 mm guns and a pair of 20 mm MG 151 cannon – a small number of 'Tonys' also had an all-cannon armament. Postwar examination of Japanese records suggest that the Ki-61 may have accounted for more P-38s in New Guinea than any of the other Japanese Army or Navy fighters in-theatre. Despite this, Lightning pilots were delighted to meet the 'Tony' in combat because it seemed heavier and less manoeuvrable than the Zero or 'Oscar'. This extra weight did, however, mean that the 'Tony' was better at chasing the P-38 in level flight or in a dive – the favoured methods of escape for USAAF pilots – than either the Mitsubishi or Nakajima fighters. Despite the Ki-61 possessing a maxi-

**The 9th FS's Thomas Fowler, Sidney Woods, Jack Mankin and Dick Bong were photographed soon after returning from a successful mission during the Battle of the Bismarck Sea on 11 March 1943. On this occasion Bong made the best of a bad manoeuvre when he turned into a formation of nine Zeros by mistake by simply flying head on into their attacking fire – he claimed two fighters shot down when he returned to base. The head on attack soon became his trademark (*US Army*)**

**Eight-kill ace Lt John Jones of the 80th FS poses by his P-38H-5 *'G.I. ANNIE'* in late 1943. The scoreboard on this aircraft also denotes kills achieved by other pilots whilst flying *'ANNIE***

mum speed of around 360 mph, the P-38 still enjoyed a margin of superiority particularly at heights above 20,000 ft. However, below this altitude many a Lightning pilot was rudely surprised to find a 'Tony' still grimly hanging onto his tail long after a Zero or an 'Oscar' had been left behind.

In spite of evidence showing a Japanese appreciation of the P-38, the fighter was held in contempt by a number of enemy pilots – the latter tended to be new to combat and with little experience of fighting the Lightning. This was primarily due to the fact that Japanese pilots believed they were scoring heavily against the P-38, when in reality few Lockheed fighters were lost in aerial combat over New Guinea or the Solomons. The truth for the Japanese pilots may have been the same as for their Axis counterparts in Germany or Italy – they simply found it hard to believe that a twin-engined fighter could compete with a single-engined machine in a close-quarters dogfight.

Not all Japanese pilots felt this way, however. In China and Burma, their opinion was far more realistic about the P-38's fighting ability. There were only two active Lightning squadrons in-theatre (the 449th and 459th FSs) between July 1943 and the autumn of 1944, but postwar statements from Japanese air intelligence officers suggest that the P-38 was perhaps the most feared Allied fighter in Burma, surpassing even the P-51, Spitfire or Mosquito as the most dreaded aerial foe. The quality and morale of the handful of Lightning pilots in the CBI was a contributing factor in the creation of this legend, and the squadrons produced nine aces between them, plus others with many aircraft claimed as destroyed on the ground.

American appreciation of the P-38 was certainly widespread, with crews in the South and South-west Pacific, the CBI and, on a smaller scale, in the Central Pacific giving high praise to the performance and ease of maintenance attributed to the machine. Pilots who had converted onto the Lockheed fighter from the P-39, P-40 or P-47 may have had fond memories of their former machines, but life in the P-38 became even sweeter over the broad expanses of the Pacific Ocean, with missions being flown from rough bases against an enemy who had little chance against a seasoned Lightning flight.

One fighter that could perhaps have rivalled the success of the Lightning in-theatre was the P-51. All the advantages (range, speed and reliability) that the Mustang enjoyed in Europe were applicable to missions in the Pacific, but those few disadvantages suffered by the fighter were magnified in the latter theatre. For example, one factor that severely limited the P-51's success in the Philippines was that it

proved too fragile to operate from the rough runways employed during this campaign. Therefore, the bulk of the fighter missions flown were performed by the P-38, which easily claimed the lion's share of kills throughout the early months of 1945 primarily because its landing gear was much more adaptable to the hastily-laid airstrips of Luzon! It was only after Clark Field had been secured in the spring of 1945 that the P-51 was finally cleared to operate from a forward base.

The P-38 was also more suited to long overwater missions thanks to its twin-engine safety factor and outstanding range. Although P-51 pilots were able to stay with the Allied bombers on all but the very longest of missions, they never really felt as much at ease with a single liquid-cooled engine powering them over those great blue expanses of the Pacific as did a P-38 pilot sandwiched between two Allison powerplants. These factors, allied with its superlative combat record in the hands of pilots like Bong, McGuire and Westbrook, made the P-38 the fighter of choice in this theatre of operations right up until VJ-Day.

## THE L FACTOR

The P-38L was issued to Pacific units during the second half of 1944, and despite having dive flaps and power-boosted controls, it was received

Capt Ken Ladd's P-38J wore nose-art typical of that favoured by many of the young and aggressive fighter pilots that comprised the 80th FS. It was photographed in the summer of 1944
(*Howard Dean via Larry Hickey*)

Capt Kenneth Hart of the 431st FS was one of the few P-38 pilots to score all of his kills on the L-model Lightning. This gaudy L-5(44-25863), nicknamed *PEEWEE V*, was assigned to the Californian ace sometime after he had downed his final two kills on 28 March 1945, which took his score to eight

Col 'Mac' MacDonald and Charles Lindbergh pose in front of the former's P-38J-15 42-104024 – nicknamed *PUTT PUTT MARU* like all of his other aircraft – at Biak in mid-July 1944. As previously mentioned, Lindbergh actually downed a Japanese aircraft during his two-month spell with MacDonald's 475th FG, this success resulting in the group's commanding officer being recalled to the USA to serve out a three-month suspension for allowing his strictly non-combatant guest to engage the enemy (*Dennis G Cooper*)

rather indifferently by seasoned frontline pilots in-theatre. Combat veterans knew that the P-38 could never be made as manoeuvrable as any of the Japanese fighters, and so had abandoned the turning fight with the enemy in favour of high speed bounces and zoom climbs. This reduced the value of the power-assisted ailerons, making them more of a luxury than a necessity. In respect to the dive flaps, squadron commanders within the Fifth Air Force had to caution their young pilots not to use them to increase the P-38's manoeuvrability, and thus attempt to dogfight with a Japanese fighter. These flaps had been fitted principally to eradicate the compressibility problems that had plagued the P-38 when diving at speed from high altitude whilst chasing Luftwaffe fighters over Europe – never a problem in the Pacific, where most combats involving the Lightning occurred at below 15,000 ft. In point of fact at least one P-38 ace – Capt 'Kenny' Giroux of the 36th FS – was convinced that the P-38 could reach 600+ mph indicated in a dive! There is no record of him actually attempting to achieve this speed in a Lightning.

When all was said and done in respect to the merits and failings of the

The number 100 was seemingly reserved for the CO's aircraft within the 475th FG, for when Lt Col John Loisel assumed command of the group from 'Mac' MacDonald in July 1945, his P-38L became 'Blue 100' in place of *PUTT PUTT MARU*. Loisel had scored one of the last victories achieved by the 475th FG on 28 March 1945 when he downed an expertly-handled Ki-84 'Frank' (*via Jeffrey Ethell*)

P-38 in the Pacific, two factors stood out that all fighter pilots agreed upon – the aircraft possessed daunting firepower and spectacular performance in the climb. The 432nd FS's Capt Joe Forster had nine victories to his credit when he was posted back to the US for command training in early 1945. As part of his course he gave a lecture on the merits of the P-38 to a group of newly-trained Mustang pilots. Just as he was leaving the auditorium he heard the next speaker, who was obviously a P-51 advocate, advise the listeners to totally disregard everything they had just heard about the climb rate of the P-38.

Forster immediately turned on his heels and challenged the speaker to a mock combat, which the latter immediately accepted. Later that day the P-51 and P-38 pilots taxied out to the runway and prepared to settle the argument once and for all. Forster knew that he could get the drop on his challenger from the minute they began their take-off runs as the P-38 could use virtually full power from brakes off thanks to the neutralised torque of its props, which rotated in opposite directions.

The pilot in the single-engined P-51 had no such advantage, and therefore had to gradually feed on the power in order to avoid the vicious swing associated with excessive prop torque on take-off. Forster exploited his advantage to the full, building up enough revs prior to releasing the brakes to take-off almost vertically in comparison with the P-51! For the next few minutes the Lightning dominated the floundering Mustang with mock passes from above. When the two fighters eventually flew combat against each other from an equal start at altitude, the superb Mustang easily prevailed, but the first few moments of this sortie had taught the P-51 pilot to respect the climbing ability of the P-38.

**36th FS CO Capt Don Campbell was photographed en route to Halmahera in his P-38J by the unit's ranking ace Capt William 'Kenny' Giroux in the latter part of 1944. Note the external drop tanks snugly fitted between the engines and the fuselage – a standard fit on Pacific theatre P-38s (*Giroux*)**

**80th FS CO Capt Jay T Robbins claimed five Japanese fighters during the Hollandia missions in March and April 1944, taking his score up to 18 confirmed kills. Having flown throughout the spring in the hotly contested skies over Hollandia, P-38J-15 *JANDINA III* was finally written off in a wheels up landing near Saidor on 7 May 1944**

# COLOUR PLATES

This 15-page colour section profiles many of the aircraft flown by the leading Lightning aces in the Pacific and CBI, as well as some of the lesser known pilots who scored five or more kills. All the artwork has been specially commissioned for this volume, and profile artist Tom Tullis and figure artist Mike Chappell have gone to great pains to illustrate the aircraft and their pilots as accurately as possible following in-depth research. Almost all of the Lightnings depicted over the following pages have never been illustrated in colour before, and the schemes shown have been fully authenticated by surviving P-38 pilots from the 1942-45 period.

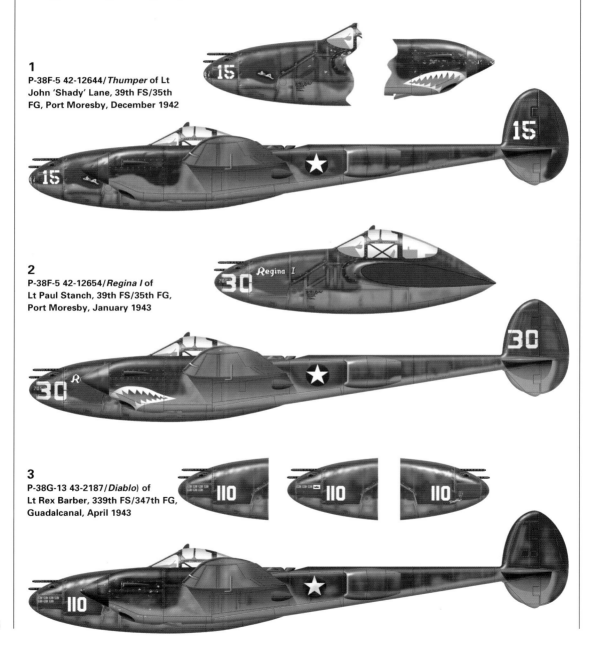

**1**
**P-38F-5 42-12644/*Thumper* of Lt John 'Shady' Lane, 39th FS/35th FG, Port Moresby, December 1942**

**2**
**P-38F-5 42-12654/*Regina I* of Lt Paul Stanch, 39th FS/35th FG, Port Moresby, January 1943**

**3**
**P-38G-13 43-2187/*Diablo*) of Lt Rex Barber, 339th FS/347th FG, Guadalcanal, April 1943**

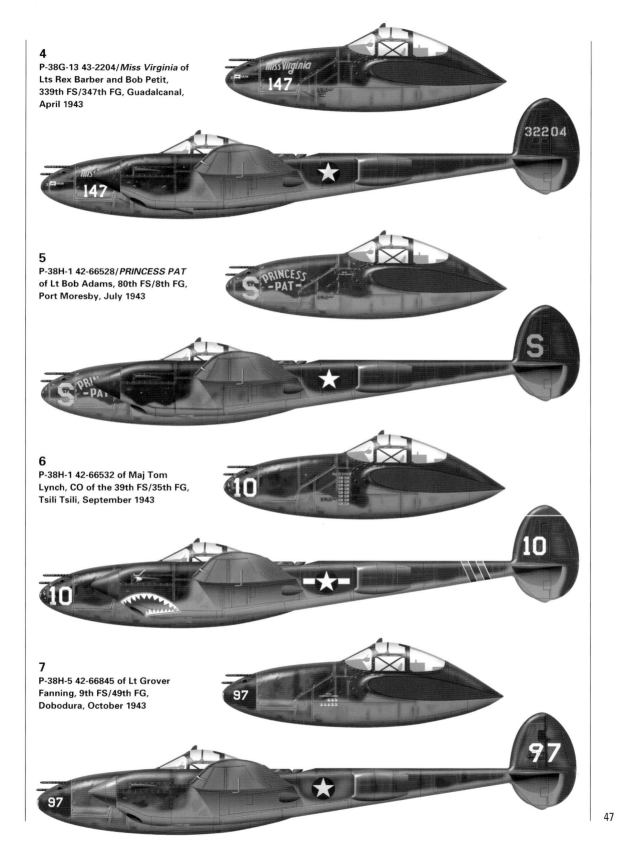

**4**
P-38G-13 43-2204/*Miss Virginia* of
Lts Rex Barber and Bob Petit,
339th FS/347th FG, Guadalcanal,
April 1943

**5**
P-38H-1 42-66528/*PRINCESS PAT*
of Lt Bob Adams, 80th FS/8th FG,
Port Moresby, July 1943

**6**
P-38H-1 42-66532 of Maj Tom
Lynch, CO of the 39th FS/35th FG,
Tsili Tsili, September 1943

**7**
P-38H-5 42-66845 of Lt Grover
Fanning, 9th FS/49th FG,
Dobodura, October 1943

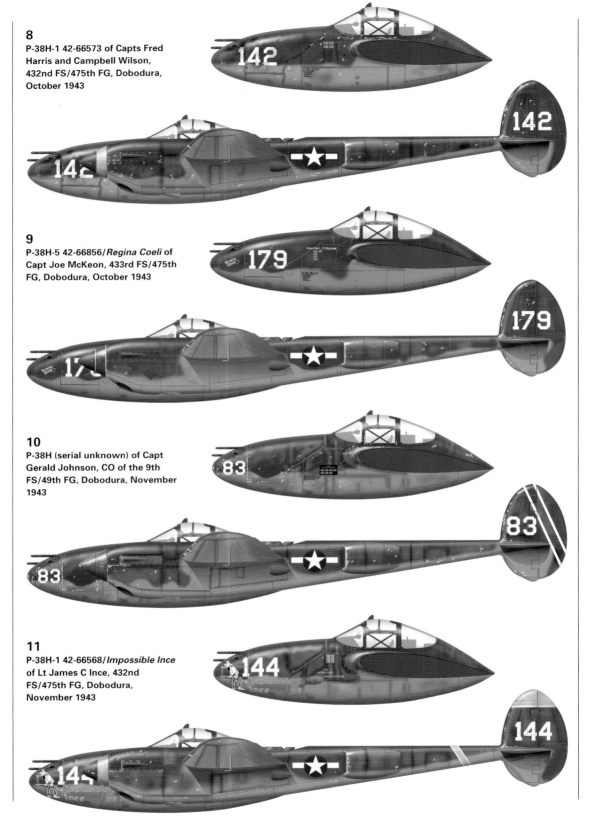

**8**
P-38H-1 42-66573 of Capts Fred
Harris and Campbell Wilson,
432nd FS/475th FG, Dobodura,
October 1943

**9**
P-38H-5 42-66856/*Regina Coeli* of
Capt Joe McKeon, 433rd FS/475th
FG, Dobodura, October 1943

**10**
P-38H (serial unknown) of Capt
Gerald Johnson, CO of the 9th
FS/49th FG, Dobodura, November
1943

**11**
P-38H-1 42-66568/*Impossible Ince*
of Lt James C Ince, 432nd
FS/475th FG, Dobodura,
November 1943

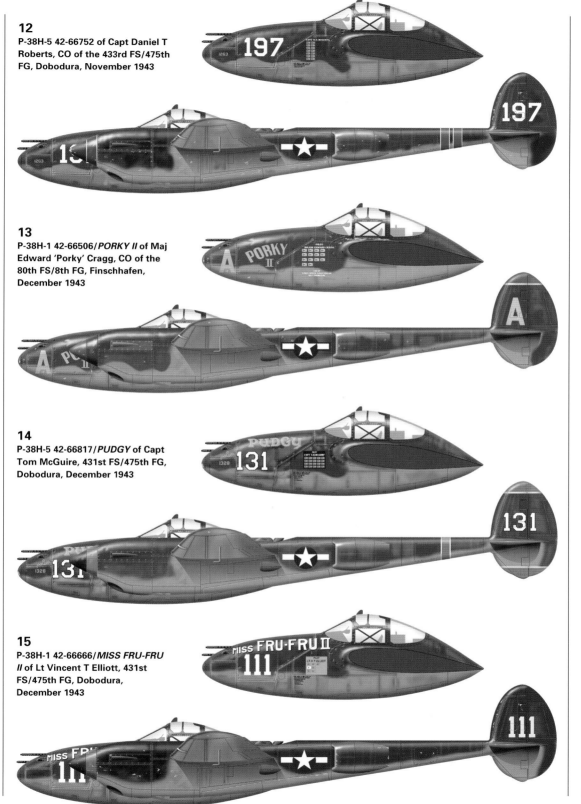

**12**
P-38H-5 42-66752 of Capt Daniel T
Roberts, CO of the 433rd FS/475th
FG, Dobodura, November 1943

**13**
P-38H-1 42-66506/*PORKY II* of Maj
Edward 'Porky' Cragg, CO of the
80th FS/8th FG, Finschhafen,
December 1943

**14**
P-38H-5 42-66817/*PUDGY* of Capt
Tom McGuire, 431st FS/475th FG,
Dobodura, December 1943

**15**
P-38H-1 42-66666/*MISS FRU-FRU
II* of Lt Vincent T Elliott, 431st
FS/475th FG, Dobodura,
December 1943

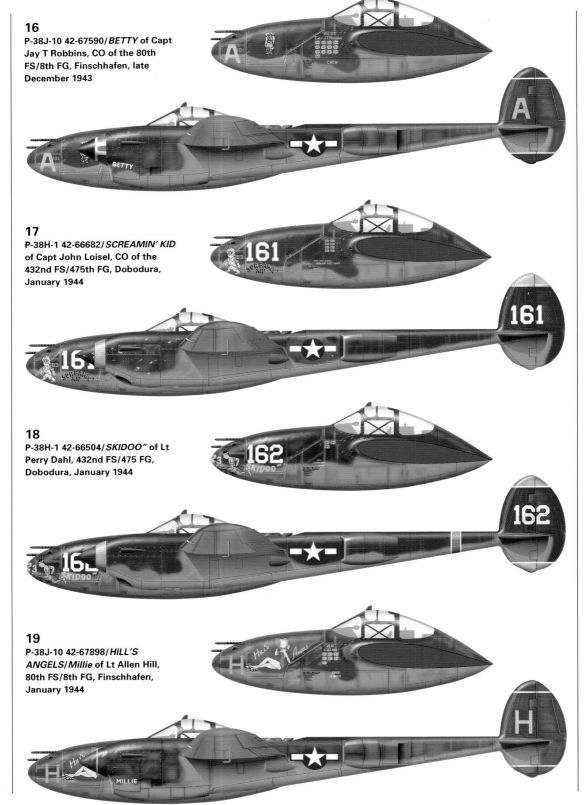

**16**
P-38J-10 42-67590/*BETTY* of Capt
Jay T Robbins, CO of the 80th
FS/8th FG, Finschhafen, late
December 1943

**17**
P-38H-1 42-66682/*SCREAMIN' KID*
of Capt John Loisel, CO of the
432nd FS/475th FG, Dobodura,
January 1944

**18**
P-38H-1 42-66504/*SKIDOO"* of Lt
Perry Dahl, 432nd FS/475 FG,
Dobodura, January 1944

**19**
P-38J-10 42-67898/*HILL'S
ANGELS/Millie* of Lt Allen Hill,
80th FS/8th FG, Finschhafen,
January 1944

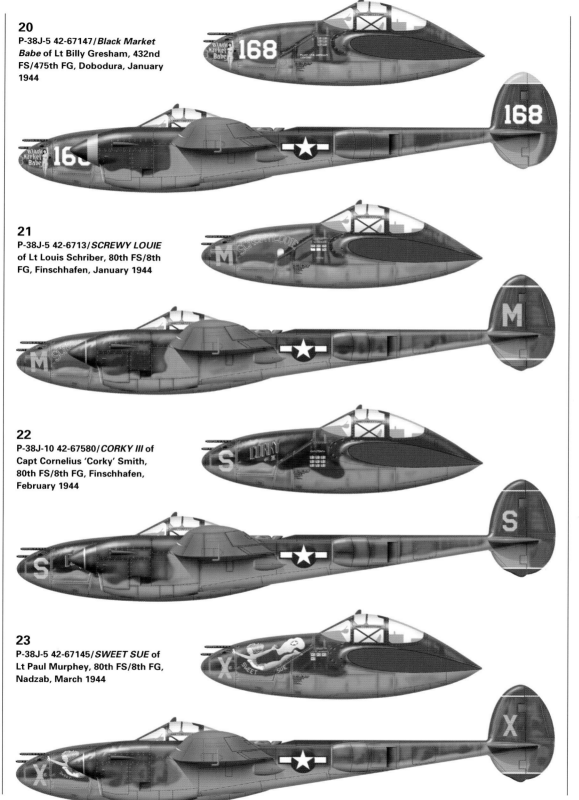

**20**
P-38J-5 42-67147/*Black Market Babe* of Lt Billy Gresham, 432nd FS/475th FG, Dobodura, January 1944

**21**
P-38J-5 42-6713/*SCREWY LOUIE* of Lt Louis Schriber, 80th FS/8th FG, Finschhafen, January 1944

**22**
P-38J-10 42-67580/*CORKY III* of Capt Cornelius 'Corky' Smith, 80th FS/8th FG, Finschhafen, February 1944

**23**
P-38J-5 42-67145/*SWEET SUE* of Lt Paul Murphey, 80th FS/8th FG, Nadzab, March 1944

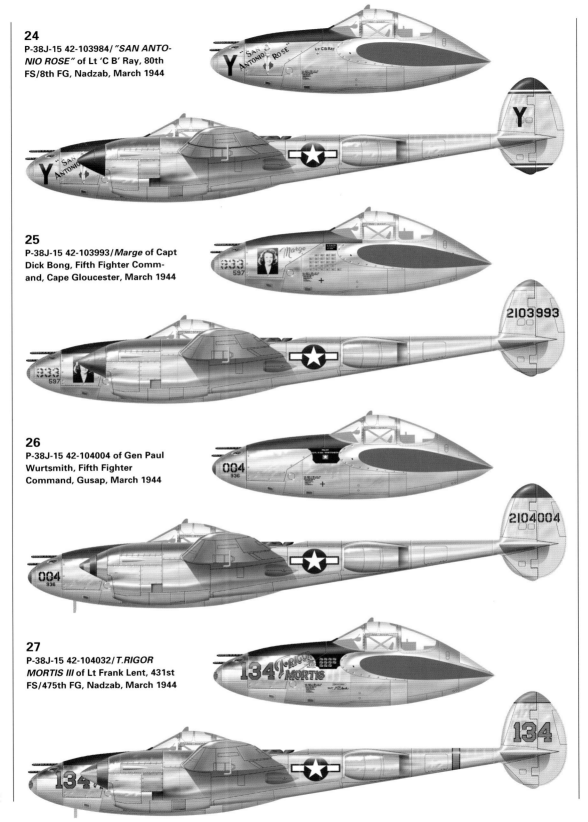

**24**
P-38J-15 42-103984/*"SAN ANTO-NIO ROSE"* of Lt 'C B' Ray, 80th FS/8th FG, Nadzab, March 1944

**25**
P-38J-15 42-103993/*Marge* of Capt Dick Bong, Fifth Fighter Command, Cape Gloucester, March 1944

**26**
P-38J-15 42-104004 of Gen Paul Wurtsmith, Fifth Fighter Command, Gusap, March 1944

**27**
P-38J-15 42-104032/*T.RIGOR MORTIS III* of Lt Frank Lent, 431st FS/475th FG, Nadzab, March 1944

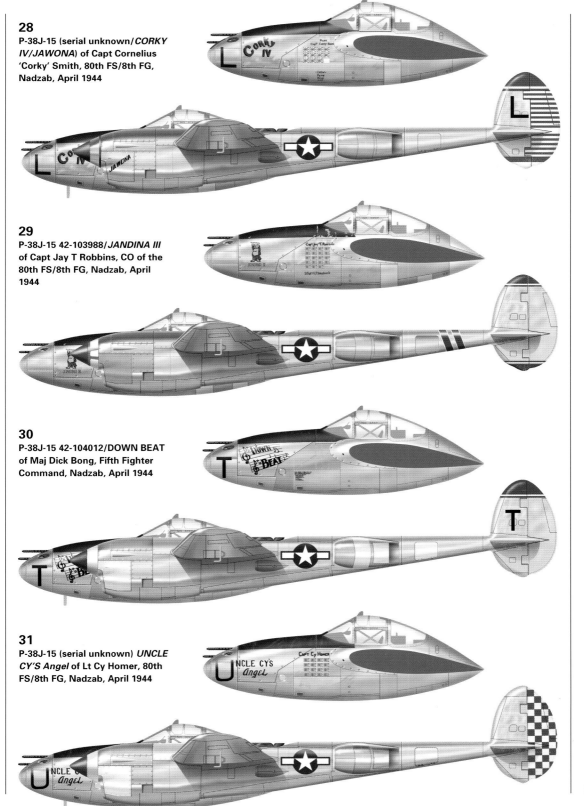

**28**
P-38J-15 (serial unknown/*CORKY IV/JAWONA*) of Capt Cornelius 'Corky' Smith, 80th FS/8th FG, Nadzab, April 1944

**29**
P-38J-15 42-103988/*JANDINA III* of Capt Jay T Robbins, CO of the 80th FS/8th FG, Nadzab, April 1944

**30**
P-38J-15 42-104012/DOWN BEAT of Maj Dick Bong, Fifth Fighter Command, Nadzab, April 1944

**31**
P-38J-15 (serial unknown) *UNCLE CY'S Angel* of Lt Cy Homer, 80th FS/8th FG, Nadzab, April 1944

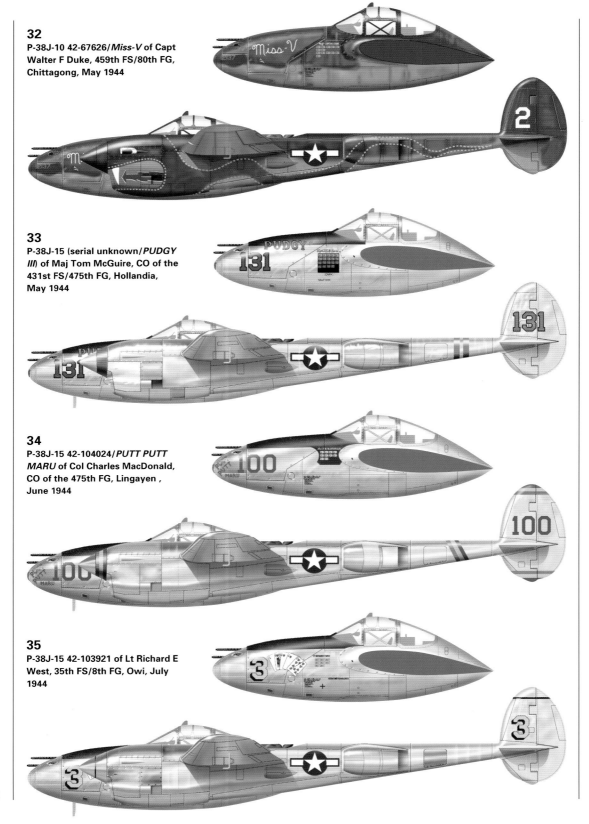

**32**
P-38J-10 42-67626/*Miss-V* of Capt Walter F Duke, 459th FS/80th FG, Chittagong, May 1944

**33**
P-38J-15 (serial unknown/*PUDGY III*) of Maj Tom McGuire, CO of the 431st FS/475th FG, Hollandia, May 1944

**34**
P-38J-15 42-104024/*PUTT PUTT MARU* of Col Charles MacDonald, CO of the 475th FG, Lingayen , June 1944

**35**
P-38J-15 42-103921 of Lt Richard E West, 35th FS/8th FG, Owi, July 1944

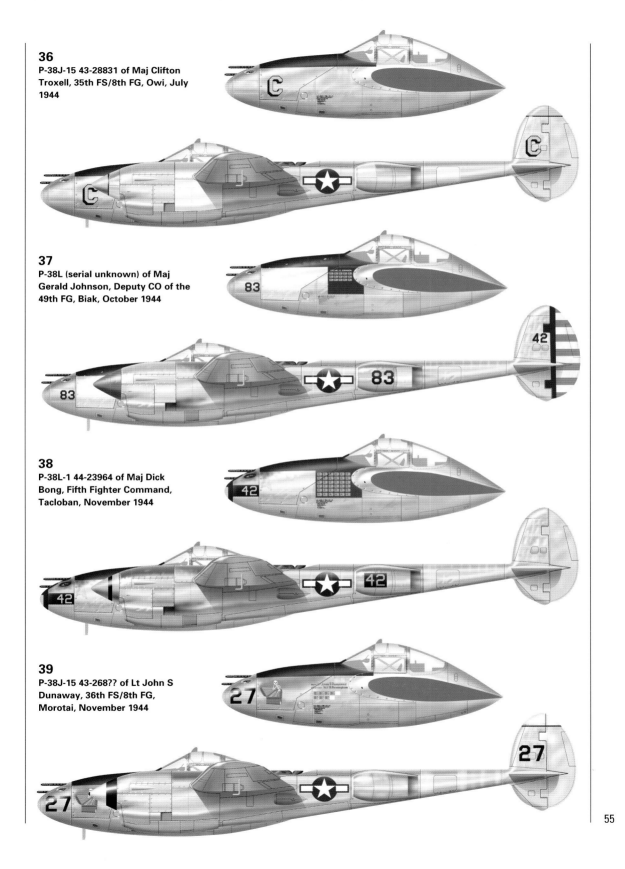

**36**
P-38J-15 43-28831 of Maj Clifton
Troxell, 35th FS/8th FG, Owi, July
1944

**37**
P-38L (serial unknown) of Maj
Gerald Johnson, Deputy CO of the
49th FG, Biak, October 1944

**38**
P-38L-1 44-23964 of Maj Dick
Bong, Fifth Fighter Command,
Tacloban, November 1944

**39**
P-38J-15 43-268?? of Lt John S
Dunaway, 36th FS/8th FG,
Morotai, November 1944

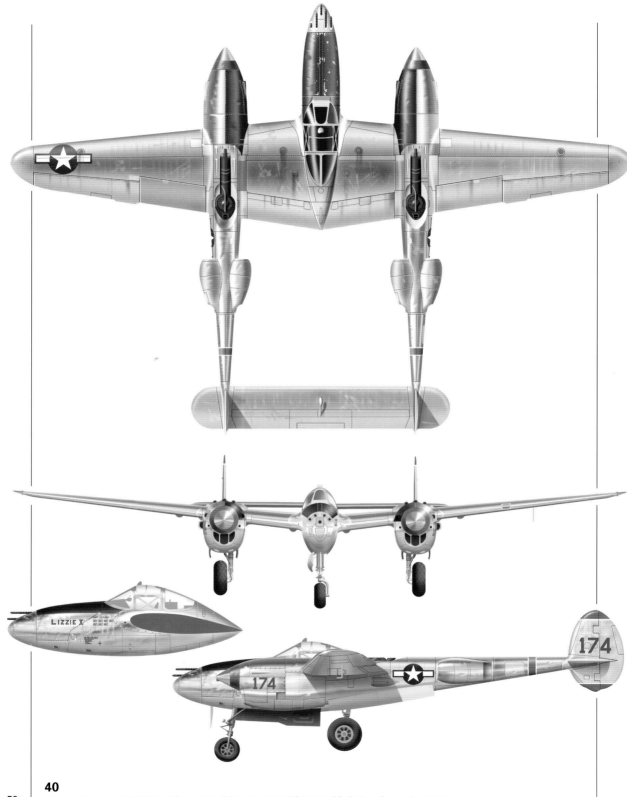

**40**

P-38L-5 44-25930/*LIZZIE V* of Capt John E Purdy, 433rd FS/475th FG, Dulag, December 1944

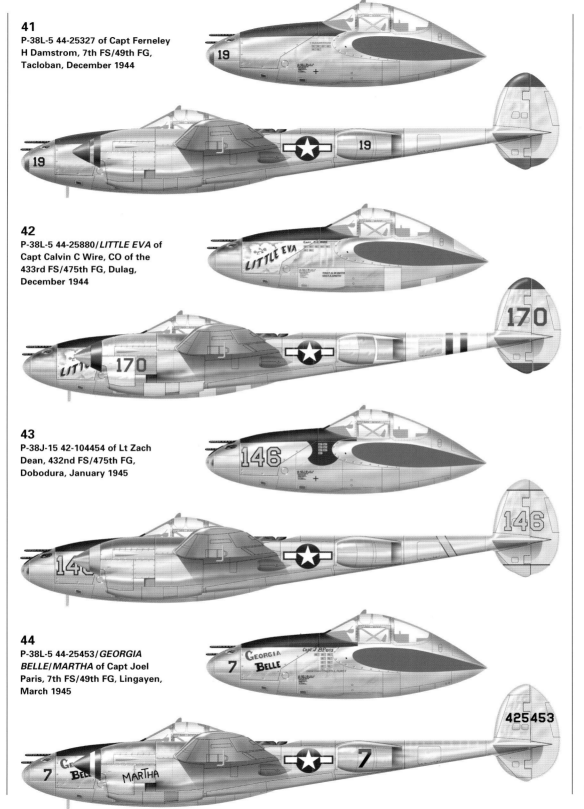

**41**
P-38L-5 44-25327 of Capt Ferneley
H Damstrom, 7th FS/49th FG,
Tacloban, December 1944

**42**
P-38L-5 44-25880/*LITTLE EVA* of
Capt Calvin C Wire, CO of the
433rd FS/475th FG, Dulag,
December 1944

**43**
P-38J-15 42-104454 of Lt Zach
Dean, 432nd FS/475th FG,
Dobodura, January 1945

**44**
P-38L-5 44-25453/*GEORGIA
BELLE/MARTHA* of Capt Joel
Paris, 7th FS/49th FG, Lingayen,
March 1945

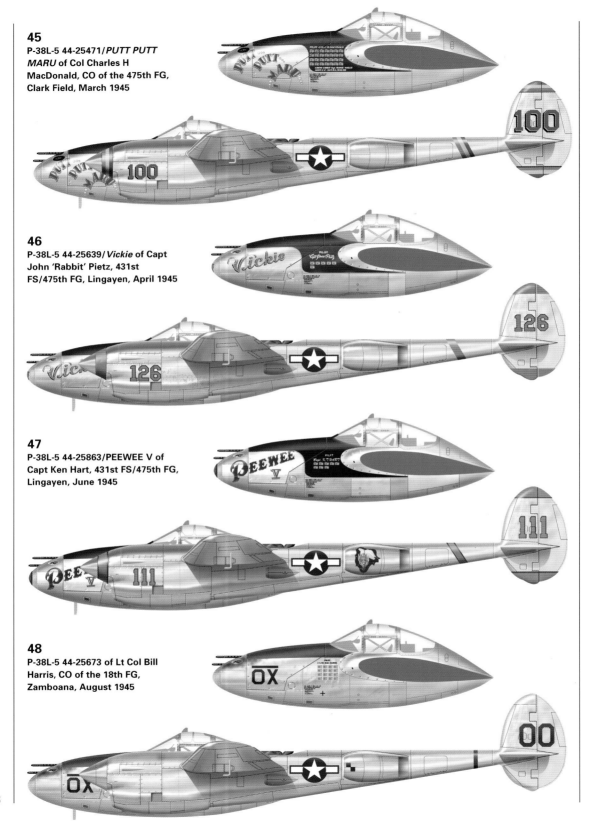

**45**
P-38L-5 44-25471/*PUTT PUTT MARU* of Col Charles H MacDonald, CO of the 475th FG, Clark Field, March 1945

**46**
P-38L-5 44-25639/*Vickie* of Capt John 'Rabbit' Pietz, 431st FS/475th FG, Lingayen, April 1945

**47**
P-38L-5 44-25863/PEEWEE V of Capt Ken Hart, 431st FS/475th FG, Lingayen, June 1945

**48**
P-38L-5 44-25673 of Lt Col Bill Harris, CO of the 18th FG, Zamboana, August 1945

**1**
Lt Allen Hill, 80th FS/8th FG,
Finschhafen, January 1944

**2**
Capt James 'Duckbutt' Watkins, 49th
FG, Lingayen, March 1945

**3**
Maj Ed 'Porky' Cragg, CO 80th FS/8th
FG, Finschhafen, December 1943

**4**
Lt Col Robert Westbrook, Deputy CO
347th FG, Middleburg, September
1944

**5**
Lt Dick Bong, 9th FS/49th FG,
Dobodura, April 1943

**6**
Maj Tom McGuire, CO 431st FS/475th
FG, Biak, October 1944

# THE PHILIPPINES

**M**aj Tom McGuire was leading his 431st FS on a ferry mission to the newly-secured airfield at Tacloban, on the Philippine island of Leyte, on 1 November 1944 when a fighter controller at the base signalled that a red alert was in progress south of the island. The 17 P-38L-1s being flown by the unit were actually destined for the 49th FG, and despite having been briefed simply to deliver the factory-fresh Lightnings to the latter unit, McGuire sensed that this alert would be his best chance to see action for the present – he had only claimed three aircraft destroyed since July. 'Mac' quickly agreed to lead his fighters in a patrol of the area until their fuel became exhausted.

Upon reaching the grid co-ordinates given to them by Tacloban control, the 431st spotted a solitary Ki-44 'Tojo' whose pilot wisely decided to turn around and head for the clouds when he saw all the P-38s in the area. Sadly for him he had made his decision a fraction too late as the determined McGuire doggedly latched onto the Ki-44's tail and shot it down in a matter of seconds – the 'Tojo' was his 25th victory. A grinning P-38 ace climbed down from his fighter after finally completing the ferrying sortie to Tacloban, and immediately expressed his delight at the necessity of having to shoot his way into his own air base!

This brief combat marked the start of a hectic two months of action for the P-38 units in the South-west Pacific. Between 1 November and the end of 1944 over 400 victories would be credited to the Lightning, this eight-weeks of near-constant aerial combat being the last great period of scoring for the P-38 and its ace pilots. Indeed, by the time the savage Philippines campaign finally ground to a halt in the early spring of 1945, the last Lightning aces of the war would have been generated.

The pace of combat in this theatre can be judged by simply examining the operational record of the 49th FG during the opening stages of the invasion. Their first kill of the campaign was achieved on 29 October when future ace Lt Milden Mathre of the 7th FS claimed his first kill (an 'Oscar') and the 49th's 500th. Less than six weeks later on 7 December, Deputy CO of the group, Maj Jerry Johnson, had his best day in action when he quickly accounted for three 'Oscars' and a Ki-49 'Helen' bomber (to take his score to 21), one of which was later recognised as being the 49th's 600th victory.

Returning to the early encounters of the invasion, Lt Ernie Ambort was one of the 9th FS aces who

'Kenny' Giroux (right) and Dick West are seen in front of the former's P-38J (nicknamed *Whilma II/Dead Eye Daisy*) just at about the time of the 8th FG's move from Owi to Morotai in September 1944. Both aces were good friends throughout their tour of combat, even though they served in different squadrons within the group – West was in the 35th FS and Giroux the 36th. Both were outstanding fighter pilots, topping the kill tallies in their respective units, and both enjoyed rich pickings over the Philippines between 1 and 15 November 1944 – Giroux claimed eight Japanese fighters and West six (*Giroux*)

**Tom McGuire also did well in November 1944 whilst leading the 431st over the Philippines, downing a 'Tojo', an 'Oscar' and two 'Jacks' in a 12-day period at the start of the month. He is seen here in P-38L-1 44-24155 _PUDGY (V)_ soon after scoring his 25th kill (the 'Tojo' downed on 1 November en route to Leyte)**

scored his first victory on 31 October when he caught a 'Val' dive-bomber over Leyte. His tally rose quickly during the next weeks thanks to the destruction of a 'Tojo' in the Ormoc area on 2 November, another 'Val' plus an 'Oscar' over southern Leyte on 5 December, and finally a 'Zeke' east of Ponson Island, in Ormoc Bay, two days later.

November had opened like a whirlwind for the P-38 pilots, with 25 Japanese aircraft being claimed as shot down for the loss of the 7th FS's Capt Elliott Dent on the 1st of the month. The latter's P-38 had been hit by AA fire from a destroyer in Ormoc Bay, and through great skill, Dent had managed to put the stricken fighter down in a mangrove swamp. He was recovered from here a fortnight later. Incidentally, Dent was the high scoring pilot of the day, his three Zeros combining with his previous trio of scores on P-40K/Ns to make him a six-kill ace. This was his last combat mission of the war, as his orders to return to America were issued whilst he was still lying low in the mangrove swamp.

Another long-serving 9th FS P-38 pilot who made ace in a matter of weeks over the Philippines was Lt Cheatham Gupton, an affable young native of North Carolina. His first two victories were 'Vals' on 1 November, whilst his last three were 'Oscars', the final one of which was scored near Tacloban on 26 November to make him an ace.

Yet another 49th FG ace to claim his premier kill on 1 November was Lt Nial Castle, who had managed to lose his leader in 'Racoon Red Flight' (of the 8th FS) during the course of a swirling dogfight west of Duljugan Point, on the Leyte coast. Realising that a single Lightning in a combat area stood little chance against superior numbers of Japanese fighters, Castle decided to latch onto another P-38 in the only place he knew he could definitely find one – in the middle of the main fight! Whilst flying into the dogfight in search of a wingman, he encountered an unwary Japanese fighter that he later identified as a Zero Model 52 and shot it down in flames – a nearby 7th FS pilot observed the stricken aircraft hit the water. Another Zero promptly attacked Castle, who simply turned into the attack and hit his assailant in the fuel tank with a deadly accurate burst. The Mitsubishi fighter exploded less than 300 ft away from Castle's P-38. By this time the lone pilot realised that his original plan may have been somewhat flawed in light of the opposition in the area, so instead he went into cloud and headed for home.

The following day saw even more Japanese aircraft in the Ormoc Bay area, resulting in P-38 claims of over 30 aircraft shot down. The 36th FS's Capt Kenny Giroux of high speed diving fame (chapter four) started his impressive scoring bout with the P-38J-20 when he downed three A6M3 'Hamps' in just a few minutes during an early afternoon sortie. Future ace Lt Fernley Damstrom of the 7th FS scored his first kill (an 'Oscar') later that day, whilst 8th FS CO Capt Bill Drier led 'Racoon Red Flight' into a dogfight over the Ormoc area that resulted in him claiming an 'Oscar' and two Zeros for his first kills of the war.

Drier was presented with just one more scoring opportunity some 22 days later whilst patrolling Caragara Bay with his Ops Officer, Capt Bob Aschenbrener. During the course of the early-morning sortie they ran

This quartet of pilots accounted for six victories between them during a mission to Balikpapan on 10 October 1944, Dick Bong (left) claiming two of them to take his score to 30. The major was flying with the 9th FS on this occasion, and the unit's CO, Maj Wallace 'Stitch' Jordan, can be seen leaning on Bong's shoulder. Jordan also 'bagged' two kills on this sortie, giving him ace status – he claimed a further victory four days later to take his final tally to six, five of which had been achieved in P-38s. Capt Edward Howes, who came close to 'making ace' with four victories and a probable (including an 'Oscar' on this mission), is standing next to Jordan, whilst to his left is Lt Warren Curton, who claimed his second kill during the Balikpapan sortie. The latter went on to score his fifth, and last, victory over Leyte on 5 December 1944

into a large force of 'Tonys', 'Oscars' and Zekes. Undaunted by the enemy's numerical superiority, the pair had succeeded in downing seven fighters (Aschenbrener had claimed three 'Tonys' and a Zeke, whilst Drier bagged two and one respectively) by the time more P-38s from the 8th FS arrived on the scene. During the course of this memorable combat, both men had become aces. Aschenbrener had already scored three victories whilst flying P-40Ns with the 8th over New Guinea in 1943/44, and he would go on to claim another 'Tony' on 28 November for his fifth P-38 victory – he finally finished the war with ten kills.

The 475th FG was also in action on the 24th, and a number of the victories recorded on this date around Leyte had some significance to the story of the P-38 aces. Capt Paul Lucas had joined the 432nd FS in July 1943, but had scored just a solitary kill (on 21 August 1943 flying P-38H 42-66555) during his 16 months with the unit. This all changed during the morning patrol west of Tacloban, for his flight of P-38L-1s engaged a formation of 'Tonys' and he swiftly shot two of them down. Three days later he would claim two more Zeros over Leyte to achieve ace status.

Lts Ken Hart and John 'Rabbit' Pietz of the 431st FS were also out on the early morning patrol on the 24th when they encountered Japanese fighters near Carigara. Hart claimed two 'Tonys' while Pietz got two 'Oscars' for their first victories. Later that same morning Pietz shot down a 'Kate' torpedo bomber in P-38L-1 44-24871, whilst on his second mission for the day Hart bagged a 'Jake' floatplane during an afternoon patrol. Both pilots would go on to score their fifth kills before the end of December.

## THE 'BIG SHOW'

The month-long fighting in November had seen most Japanese units lose a great number of their experienced fighter pilots in action over the Philippines. In the Leyte and Cebu areas many aircraft from the Clark Field-based 203rd and 653rd Air Groups had been shot down whilst trying to stem the near constant bombing and strafing raids undertaken by Allied squadrons in support of the invasion. For example, in the first 48 hours of the month the Japanese lost CPOs Tsunesaku Saki, Shoji Kato

**Lt Col Robert 'Westy' Westbrook was the Thirteenth AF's leading ace of World War 2, having downed 20 aircraft by the time he was shot down and killed during a strafing mission over the Celebes on 22 November 1944. Deputy CO of the 347th FG at the time of his death, he had claimed his final trio of kills (all 'Oscars') on 23 October whilst leading the group on an attack on Boeloedowang airfield. The Thirteenth carried out much strafing and ground attack work in 1944/45**

**This photo-call at Tacloban in October 1944 saw all available 9th FS pilots who weren't flying at the time swarm around Dick Bong's P-38L-1 44-23964 for an official shot for the scrapbook. Bong claimed at least five kills in this Lightning over the Philippines (Cheatham Gupton)**

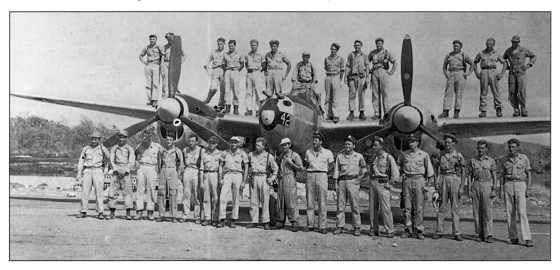

and Chozo Nakaya, all of whom had been flying Zeros with these units since the early days.

The end of November saw a gradual lessening of the intensity of air combat over the Leyte area, the Allies taking stock of the campaign so far. On the ground there had been less progress than originally envisaged, resulting in another landing being scheduled for the Ormoc Bay sector in the hope of crushing the stiff Japanese resistance being encountered in this region. The amphibious assault took place virtually unopposed on 7 December, thanks primarily to several days of aerial activity over the area.

All P-38 assets were involved in the build-up to the 'Big Show', and one pilot who scored heavily on either side of D-Day was Lt John Purdy of the 433rd FS. A native of Detroit, Purdy had been in-theatre since the end of 1943, but had only scored a solitary kill (an 'Oscar' on 16 May) up to this point in his combat tour. Despite his lack of success against the enemy, Purdy was rated by his peers as one of the most aggressive pilots in the whole unit. He got to release some of this pent up aggression on a pair of 'Vals' he intercepted near Cebu town late in the afternoon of 5 December. This double success was repeated six days later when Purdy destroyed a pair of 'Oscars' and damaged a third – he was forced to crash land his P-38L-5 on Cabugan Grande Island after it ran out of fuel following this engagement. Finally, on 17 December Purdy scored his last kills, which comprised a pair of Zeke Model 52s over the newly-invaded island of Mindoro. He finished the war with a score of seven confirmed, two probables and one damaged.

As mentioned earlier, Ken Hart made ace at around this time, shooting down a 'Val' near Ormoc on 2 December for his fourth victory and destroying a pair of 'Oscars' whilst covering the amphibious assault five days later. Fellow 431st FS pilot, and close rival, John Pietz had to wait until Christmas Day to make ace by claiming two relatively rare J2M3 'Jack' fighters just north of Clark Field.

On the day the Ormoc landings were made, the biggest aerial clash of the entire Philippines campaign involving the P-38 was fought overhead. More than 50 Japanese aircraft were claimed destroyed for the loss of just a single Lightning and its pilot. However, that one loss was acutely felt in the P-38 community for it was none other than ex-475th FG CO, Lt Col Meryl M Smith. The seasoned Lightning ace had just shot down his eighth and ninth kills (two 'Jacks') when his P-38L-1 (44-23945) was jumped and he was shot down over Ormoc Bay. Smith's body was never found.

On a more positive note, the 7th FS's Fernley Damstrom built on his early successes of the previous month by 'making ace' in style through the destruction of two 'Nicks' and a Zero on 7 December. In his combat report for this sortie Damstrom recorded the harrowing experience of watching another Japanese fighter that he could not intercept make a suicide attack on a destroyer that left the vessel both dead in the water and badly ablaze. He had been leading 'Pinky Blue Flight' on a cover mission over the convoy at the time, and aside from witnessing one of the first *Kamikaze* strikes of the war, had also spotted two Zeros below his formation trying to slip in on the tails of other P-38s from the 7th FS. Damstrom swiftly negated this threat by setting one of the A6Ms alight thanks to an accurate burst of tracer fire that hit its unprotected starboard

Maj Wallace 'Stitch' Jordan poses with his P-38L-1 soon after his final kill had been marked up on its scoreboard. He was posted to the 49th FG HQ flight soon after attaining his last victory, and failed to add to his tally. Jordan earned his nickname from a prominent scar on his forehead, which was the end result of a jeep accident in New Guinea, rather than a Japanese bullet in combat!

Capt John 'Rabbit' Pietz of the 431st FS claimed two J1M 'Jack' fighters over Clark Field on Christmas Day 1944 to register his fourth and fifth air victories. He subsequently claimed an additional Ki-44 'Tojo' over the Asian mainland on 28 March 1945. This photograph shows him standing in front of P-38L-5 44-25639 *Vickie*, and was taken in mid-1945 after Pietz had made captain

65

wing root fuel tank – a favoured tactic of all Lightning pilots confronted by the staple Navy fighter.

This kill had been preceded earlier in the day by the destruction of two 'Nicks' whilst on a lengthy morning patrol over the occupied islands. Texan Damstrom was now an ace, and he would score three more victories in December before the 7th FS was moved to Laong airfield on Luzon after the invasion at Lingayen. He would also be appointed Ops Officer for his squadron shortly before he was killed in a take-off accident at Luzon in P-38L-5 44-25327 on 11 April 1945.

## CLARK FIELD

The centre of Japanese air power in the Philippines (just as it had been for the Americans in the aftermath of Pearl Harbor) was the large complex of airstrips at Clark Field, near Manila. In order to prevail over the large Japanese force entrenched across the myriad islands in the region, US airpower had to neutralise the base in much the same way as the attacking Imperial forces had done almost three years before.

The first strikes on Clark Field were flown on the afternoon of 22 December 1944, and resulted in 19 Japanese fighters being shot down by P-47Ds of the 348th FG. This outfit went on to have its best day of the war 48 hours later when it claimed more than 30 Japanese fighters destroyed over and around the airfield.

P-38s of the Fifth Air Force would have to wait until Christmas Day to be unleashed on Clark, but were nevertheless kept busy in the interim consolidating the invasion of Mindoro Island to the west of Leyte. Aside from John Purdy's successes, which were detailed earlier in this chapter, his 433rd FS squadron-mate Capt Jack Fisk (who had been stuck on four kills since 9 November 1943) claimed a Zero and a 'Jack' over south-west Mindoro to ensure his ace status. Now Capt Louis Schriber of the 80th FS also began scoring again after a lull of eight months by claiming a 'Hamp' over Mindoro on 22 December for his fourth victory.

Having secured the airspace over Mindoro, the P-38 units were assigned to protect B-24s sent to bomb Clark Field on Christmas Day. Opposing this massive raiding force was every available Japanese fighter in the area that could be made airworthy. The end result of this massive aerial engagement was the reported destruction of almost 40 Japanese fighters for the loss of five P-38s. This battle marked the zenith of Japanese airpower in the Philippines, and from that point on JAAF and Navy fighters were seen in ever decreasing numbers. Indeed, the Allied invasion of Luzon in January 1945 went virtually unopposed from the air.

More than half of the Japanese claims on 25 December were attributed to pilots from the 475th FG, who had run amok over Clark's satellite field at Mabalacat. Group

Having waited almost a year to secure his fifth kill, and thus achieve the coveted accolade of P-38 ace, Capt Fred 'Champ' Champlin of the 431st FS took full advantage of the Philippine invasion by claiming five victories in November/December to take his final tally to nine. This photograph shows his complete score on the side of P-38L-5 *EILEEN-ANNIE* in early 1945. Champlin flew 175 combat missions during his tour, which lasted almost two years, and went on to see action in both Korean and Viet Nam. Note 8th FS P-38L at the bottom left of this shot (*Champlin*)

'Rabbit' Pietz's P-38L-5 44-25639 is seen on a test flight prior to having its red 431st FS identification colours applied in early 1945

Capt Cy Homer (centre) assumed command of the 80th FS in October 1944 when Maj J T Robbins became Deputy CO of the 8th FG. The former scored just one kill whilst in command and on 10 November 1944, taking his final tally to 15. The other men in this photo are Homer's crewchief, SSgt Mel Gardner, and assistant crewchief, Sgt George Kicker

CO Col 'Mac' MacDonald shot down two 'Jacks' and a Zeke Model 52 over the airstrip whilst flying at the head of the 432nd FS. His newly-promoted Ops Officer, Maj Tom McGuire, also made his mark on this sortie, destroying three Zekes in a 15-minute spell on the periphery of Clark Field, and thus taking his score to 34. He had his sights firmly fixed on arch-rival Maj Dick Bong's tally of 40, which the American 'ace of aces' had chalked up courtesy of a final 'Oscar' kill over Mindoro on 17 December. Bong had also been awarded the Medal of Honor by Gen Douglas MacArthur just five days before his 40th victory, although as a caveat to receiving this medal he was issued orders posting him back to America, where full propaganda value for his achievements could be thoroughly exploited by the USAAF.

7th FS ace Lt Joel Paris claimed his fourth P-38 victory (and seventh overall, for he had previously scored three kills earlier in 1944 when the 7th FS was equipped with P-40Ns) on this mission, and gave tribute to both the Zero and the Japanese pilots encountered over Mabalacat;

'The Zeke 52 is a very fast and manoeuvrable aeroplane, and the pilots used it to its best advantage. They did not avoid head-on passes, and sometimes initiated these attacks themselves.'

On this occasion Paris had been leading 'Pinky Red Flight' when

The cockpit confines of the P-38 were relatively spacious in comparison to other Allied fighters like the Spitfire or the Mustang, as this shot of 15-kill ace Cy Homer clearly shows. Clothed in typically worn flying apparel that belies his position as squadron CO, Homer poses for the camera in his last P-38 (an L-1) in late 1944. Considered to be one of the best fighter pilots in the entire USAAF, Homer appears to have been little affected once in the air by a prewar motorcycle accident that impaired his walking stride when out of the cockpit

Japanese fighters bounced the four P-38s that comprised this formation, as well as the B-24s they were guarding. Paris took evasion action by immediately climbing for altitude and leading his flight over the top of the tightly-boxed formation of Liberators. Converting height into speed, 'Flight Lead' dived down onto the tail of a hapless Zero and fired a single burst at his foe. Hitting a fuel tank, the fighter exploded in to a fireball. The remaining Navy fighters were harassing both the bombers and the badly outnumbered P-38s by this stage, and although Paris fought off as many Zekes as he could until his wingman reported that he was low on gas, his earphones were still full of cries for help as he steered a course for home.

Another pilot that found himself in the thick of the action over Mabalacat on Christmas Day was 'Rabbit' Pietz, who was filling the 'last man' slot in the three-aircraft 'Green Flight' of the 431st FS. During the course of the engagement he managed to lose contact with his leader, Lt John Tilley, while falling back to cover the third man in the flight whose P-38L-1 was suffering from engine trouble. Whilst attempting to protect his ailing squadron-mate, Pietz was set upon from above by a formation of 'Jacks'. In the ensuing fight for survival, a single Japanese fighter was shot down, but the remaining six managed to line up behind the perplexed P-38 pilot to finish him off.

Despite being in a seemingly indefensible position, Pietz somehow managed to get into a firing position on the trailing 'Jack' and struck it with several well-placed bursts. The Mitsubishi fighter quickly burst into flames and crashed near Clark Field. Whilst wildly manoeuvring for his life, Pietz was rejoined by Tilley, and the pair confirmed 'Jack' kills for each other – the latter scored his fifth, and last, victory 24 hours later.

Aside from Tilley's Zeke Model 52, another 12 Japanese aircraft were claimed over Clark the next day, including four Zeros for Tom McGuire to give him his final score of 38 victories. As a postscript to this memorable sortie, he was in fact chasing what looked like being his fifth victim of the day when either fatigue or overzealousness saw his shots spray wide of the hapless Zeke, despite making several passes at the seemingly doomed fighter.

Not all pilots who had been weaned in combat on single-engined fighters were intially won over by the P-38, although one of them scored a quartet of kills to make ace on this day. Lt Sammy Pierce of the 49th FG had been ordered back into combat along with Bob Aschenbrener after both pilots had flown successful tours on P-40s (Pierce had scored three kills in the Warhawk) with the group in 1943/44. When he found out that his old unit had re-equipped with the P-38 since his time in the frontline, Pierce was less than enthusiastic about going into combat in the twin-engined Lockheed fighter. However, his four kills in 25 minutes

during the course of this sortie proved to him the superiority of the Lightning over its single-engined rivals.

Controversially, Pierce's final Zeke kill on this mission took the form of Tom McGuire's seemingly indestructible fifth victim, the former having watched with growing impatience as the major, and several other P-38 pilots in his formation, made futile attempts at downing the Japanese fighter. With a sure hand, he deftly dropped down on the unfortunate Zeke from a superior altitude, slotted in behind it, and promptly shot it down with a single burst! Pierce shrugged off the personal invective levelled at him over the airwaves by a rather peeved McGuire, who accused him of being 'a thieving interloper'.

Not all units participated in the Clark raids over Christmas and Boxing Day, however, pilots of the 80th FS being forced to miss the action due to their ongoing commitment to the defence of Mindoro. However, Hollandia veteran Lt 'C B' Ray did manage to score his two prerequisite kills to become an ace on the 29th of the month when he destroyed a 'Dinah' over Hill Field, on Mindoro, during a morning patrol, followed by a Zero that attempted to attack an Allied convoy whilst he was on his second sortie that afternoon. Squadron-mate 'Screwy' Louis Schriber lived up to his nickname 24 hours later when he stalked a formation of Zeros all alone over Mindoro. He shot up several of them before they even realised they were under attack, and at least one of the Zeros was seen to crash whilst two others broke away streaming smoke. The sole confirmed kill achieved by Schriber on this date made him an ace – it was also his final victory of the war.

Some of the last P-38 aces of World War 2 were created on 1 January 1945 during the final mission flown against Clark Field before the American landing in Lingayen Gulf. The 7th FS's Lt Milden

**This shot shows the starboard side of Ken Hart's P-38L-5 *PEEWEE V*, a port view being illustrated on page 43. The 431st FS started applying their Satan's Head badge to the Lightning's boom radiator housings towards the end of operations in the Philippines as new L-5s arrived in-theatre to replace their battle-weary L-1s**

**Newly-promoted Capt Joel Paris leans on P-38L-5 44-23453 *GEORGIA BELLE* in March 1945 soon after scoring his ninth, and last, kill – a Zero near Hainan Island on the sixth of that month. Second-ranking ace in the 7th FS, Paris had claimed his first three victories in the P-40N earlier in 1944, before downing a further five over the Philippines in the final weeks of that year in the Lightning**

Mathre got his fifth (and last) victory when he encountered a Zeke 52 over the airfield whilst flying as an escort for a formation of B-24s. Also registering a kill on this trip (his eighth out of nine in total) was veteran Lt Joel Paris, although his adversary proved to be a much tougher 'nut to crack'. Leading the 7th FS on this occasion, Paris had forced a group of Zeros into a defensive Lufbery Circle, which often proved very hazardous to break up. Nevertheless, he dived into the swirling 'wagon wheel' of Navy fighters and attacked them head-on, shooting the aileron off one Zero, which was seen to spin uncontrollably out of formation and crash. With the Lufbery Circle broken, the Japanese fighters scattered.

Nial Castle had seen much combat since his solo efforts back on 1 November, doubling his score through the destruction of a pair of Zekes on Boxing Day west of Clark Field. He now only needed a solitary kill to join that unique band of ace P-38 pilots, and on New Year's Day the opportunity presented itself. Castle too was escorting the same B-24s as Paris and Mathre, although he was part of an 8th FS flight on the opposite side of the bomber stream. He had heard the shouts that signalled contact with the enemy, and just as he was preparing to break formation and seek out the action, Castle noticed a 'Nick' closing directly on him, intent on making a head-on attack on the B-24s. The Ki-45 was about five miles away, and its crew were obviously totally unaware that they were flying on a collision course with an American fighter. Castle dropped from 8000 ft down to the tops of the clouds some 6000 ft below, thus letting the Japanese fighter pass right over him before he made a turning climb to get back onto the 'Nick's' tail – the Ki-45 was heavily armed, and was not the ideal fighter to attack head-on. Firing from below

Col 'Mac' MacDonald and his last P-38L-5 (44-25471) were photographed sometime in February 1945 after the boss of the 475th FG had downed his 27th, and final, kill on the 13th of that month. No less than 13 of these victories were achieved in patrols over the Philippines between 10 November 1944 and 1 January 1945

Two-tour veteran Lt Col Bill Harris stands in front of his well-kept P-38L-5 (44-25673) at Zamboana in August 1945. Like a number of veteran pilots, he extended his tour as CO of the 18th FG until war's end – by which time he had raised his score to 16, all but one of which had been achieved whilst flying with the 339th FS in 1943/44. This tally made him the top-scoring P-38 ace in the Thirteenth AF. Lightning pilots in the latter air force were relegated to tactical missions during the invasion of the Philippines, which effectively stopped men like Harris adding to their tallies – they had to make do with attacking rail and airfield targets in Borneo instead (*Harris*)

Another combat veteran of the Pacific campaign that remained in action well into 1945 was Lt Col Jerry Johnson, who served as Deputy CO of the 49th FG until June of that year. Bearing the name of his wife on its nose, Johnson's P-38L-5 is also adorned with his full tally of 22 kills – a score which made him the 49th FG's leading ace. His official tally was later boosted by two (at least in Fifth Air Force listings, if not in those of the Eleventh!) when probable kills he achieved against Zeros whilst flying P-39s with the 57th PS in the Aleutians in 1942 were upgraded to confirmed scores

at about 20° deflection, Castle immediately drew smoke from the right engine, which then burst into flames and caused the 'Nick' to crash about ten miles north-east of Manila.

After January 1945 the Philippines served more as an offensive base rather than an object of dispute. For the first time the Asian coast, as well as portions of the Central Pacific, could be reached by fighters and bombers of the newly-created Far East Air Force (FEAF) – the Fifth and Thirteenth Air Forces had been amalgamated within the FEAF in mid-1944.

The last victories for the 475th FG were scored along the coast of what is now Viet Nam at the end of March 1945. Appropriately, one of its founder members in the form of Maj John Loisel got his 11th victory on the 28th of that month when he surprised a pair of Ki-84 'Franks', downing one and chasing another until he was forced to break off the combat through lack of fuel. During the brief engagement, he had been impressed with both the Nakajima's speed and acceleration, not to mention its sparkling rate of climb. The 28th also saw John Pietz claim a 'Tojo' and Ken Hart two 'Hamps' in the same area for their final kills of the war.

Perhaps the last kill for a P-38 ace in World War 2 was controversially gained by Maj George Laven of the 49th FG. Fittingly, he had scored one of the first Lightning victories back in September 1942 when he downed an unidentified Japanese biplane over Kiska, in the Aleutians, whilst flying a P-38E with the 54th FS. His final kill (which may only give him a score of four, as his second victory was actually a shared claim against a moored flying boat again in the Aleutians in September 1942) was scored either on 21 June 1945 (a date given by Laven himself) or 26 April 1945, the latter date having appeared in a number of highly-respected publications including Frank Olynyk's superlative *Stars & Bars*.

In any event, Laven was out looking for targets on the island of Taiwan in his P-38L-5 when he encountered a large Japanese flying boat which he later identified as a four-engined 'Emily'. After numerous gunnery passes, he managed to bring the giant aircraft down for what is officially considered to be his fifth victory, thus making him the last Lightning ace of World War 2.

# P-38 ACES OF THE CBI

The end of the North African campaign in early 1943 brought a brief, but crucial, slackening in the seemingly insatiable demand placed on Lockheed by USAAF units for attrition replacement P-38s in the Mediterranean. This lull finally allowed the company to produce a small surplus of Lightnings, meaning that the requirements of other numbered air forces particularly in the Far East, who had been clamouring for a modern fighter with which to tackle the Japanese for over a year, could at last be fulfilled. From his base in Kunming, China, Gen Claire Chennault of American Volunteer Group (or simply 'Flying Tigers') fame had been particularly vociferous in his demands for adequate air power – indeed, so persistent were his requests that weary USAAF chiefs in Washington finally agreed to send some of their precious P-38Gs, and their even more precious pilots, to the China-Burma-India (CBI) theatre in the summer of 1943. Incredibly, these men and machines were drawn from units already in North Africa, rather than sending them out fresh from the USA.

One such individual was Maj Bob Kirtley, a veteran of the recent North African campaign with the crack 82nd FG. Not only was he given the task of imparting his combat experience with the P-38 to new pilots destined for the CBI, but he also had to organise their transportation to the Far East. Among the arrivals for conversion onto the Lightning was former University of Michigan football star Tom Harmon, who had trained as a B-25 pilot but was now looking for combat in fighters.

Coming under Kirtley's tutelage at the same time as Harmon was future P-38 ace Lt Bob Schultz, who was so mortified by the full horror of the Nazi philosophy revealed in the aftermath of World War 2 that he changed his ancestral German name to Shoals. He had taken delivery of a P-38G at the Langford Lodge staging depot, in Northern Ireland, at the end of April 1943 and flown it to Maison Blanche, on the outskirts of Algiers. Here, he was trained in the art of flying the fighter in combat conditions by veteran pilots of the 14th FG, before being declared ready to head for China on 5 July. He eventually arrived at Ling-Ling on 14 August, where he was assimilated into 'Squadron X', the melodramatic sobriquet that preceded the eventual identity of the 449th FS.

The second 449th FS P-38G flown by American football star Tom Harmon. He was flying the original *LITTLE BUTCH* when he became embroiled in the great air battle over Kiukiang on 30 October 1943 that saw eight P-38s take on over a dozen JAAF fighters. Harmon had 'bagged' two 'Oscars' before he was himself shot down and forced to trek for 32 days back to his own base. Whilst drifting down limply in his parachute, pretending to be dead, he witnessed future P-38 ace Lt Bob Schultz destroy a pair of 'Tojos', and thus open his account. The aircraft's nickname was inspired by Harmon's wife, the film star Elyse Knox, whilst the cartoon figure is bedecked in a University of Michigan football jersey that bears the former's college number (*Jim Crow*)

Bob Schultz was probably flying this
P-38G-10, nicknamed *GOLDEN
EAGLE*, during the 30 October sortie
mentioned in the previous caption.
He had flown this factory-fresh
aircraft from Africa in mid-August
1943, and continued to use it until
he went home in March 1944. Here,
TSgt DeVito and Capt Billy
Beardsley add mission symbols to
its nose in mid-1944 – the latter
individual had been allocated the
veteran Lightning upon Schultz's
departure (*USAF*)

Schultz's new unit had been constituted just 11 days before at Kunming, the bulk of its air- and groundcrew having flown into China on 25
July from fighter groups in North Africa. Within days of the arrival of the
P-38 and its crews, Gen Chennault decided to show off 'his' modern
fighter by arranging a mock combat demonstration between a Lightning
and a Warhawk. Unbeknown to the assembled crowd, and in particular
Claire Chennault and the P-38 pilot, groundcrews had specially stripped
out a P-40K for this very sortie, and given it to one of the unit's crack
combat pilots. Understandably, the Lightning was easily 'bested' by the
Warhawk, and from that point on a humiliated Chennault took a dim
view of the P-38 right up until war's end.

Prior to this one-sided 'fly off', a small number of P-38s had already
flown combat sorties over China from Ling-Ling before the end of July,
although it wasn't until the following month that the 449th achieved its
first kills. Led by ex-75th FS CO Maj Edmund Goss (who had scored six
kills in P-40s), the unit opened its account on 21 August over Hengyang
airfield with three confirmed Zero kills and two probables for the loss of
a single P-38 shot down whilst attempting a scramble take-off – one or
two other Lihghtnings were also superficially damaged in the ensuing
engagement.

Several more Zeros were claimed by the 449th during the course of a
dive-bombing mission against the docks at Canton on 9 September, a
quartet of P-38s equipped with two 500-lb bombs each making a successful run on the target in spite of opposition from the Japanese fighters.

A further kill was claimed by Lt Billy Beardsley, who encountered an enemy transport aircraft over the Chinese port and promptly shot it down. After the war it was discovered that he had actually destroyed the aircraft on which Gen Takuma Shimoyama, head of the 3rd Air Division, was a passenger, his sudden demise throwing Japanese aerial planning into disarray for some considerable period of time.

The next day another bombing mission to Canton was staged, during which former 1st FG veteran Lt Lee O Gregg scored his second P-38G victory when he shot down a Zero. His first kill had taken the form of a *Regia Aeronautica* Reggiane Re 2001, destroyed on 30 May 1943 off the coast of North Africa. He would gone on to score six kills in the CBI flying the Lightning. This initial victory was a hard one, for Gregg and his wingman found themselves up against roughly 16 Zeros, all of which appeared to be flown by highly-skilled pilots. Indeed, one of them actually managed to get onto the tail of Gregg's wingman, but the former managed to shoot him down. However, the enemy pilot had inflicted enough damage on its target prior to his fiery demise to force the badly damaged Lightning to make a belly-landing back at Kunming.

One of the costliest sorties flown by the 449th FS was yet another dive-bombing mission, but this time to Kiukiang on 30 October 1943. Eight P-38s were jumped by about a dozen 'Oscars' and 'Tojos' and four were rapidly shot down, although after recovering from the initial bounce, three of the surviving pilots claimed six of the attackers – four Ki-44s and two Ki-43s. Tom Harmon was credited with the two 'Oscars', although he was forced to bail out of his burning P-38 soon after scoring his second victory – he subsequently made a 32-day trek back to Ling-Ling.

Harmon had 'hit the silk' whilst the battle was still raging all around

**Fortunately for P-38 pilots in the CBI, the twin-boom layout of their fighter meant that it was easily recognisible to friendly troops on the ground, thus reducing the chances of the former being shot at by Allied forces. Nevertheless, every opportunity was taken to familiarise soldiers with the overall shape of the Lightning by letting them see it at close quarters. Here, Chinese troops are enjoying an encounter with a 449th FS P-38G at the unit's Kunming base in early 1944. Note the squatting soldier on the wing, studying the aircraft's special direction finder loop (*USAF*)**

him, and knowing that there had been reports of Japanese pilots strafing men in parachutes, he slumped over in his straps pretending to be dead. Somehow he managed to watch the battle whilst simultaneously convincing a number of curious Japanese fighters circling his descending parachute that he was indeed dead! Whilst floating down into a Chinese lake he saw Bob Schultz shoot down two 'Tojos' as he fought his way out of the trap.

That same month had seen the 449th transferred from the 23rd to the 51st FG, and like its previous controlling body, the latter group was also made up of three P-40-equipped squadrons. However, the dominance of the Warhawk in the CBI began to slowly wane from November onwards

Lt Harry 'Lighthorse' Sealey and his P-38H-5 of the 459th FS are seen at Nagaghuli in late 1943, prior to this pilot scoring his first combat kills. *Haleakala* is a Hawaiian phrase meaning 'House of the Sun', and although this Lightning was assigned to Sealey, he did not score any victories with it (*US Army*)

Lt Sealey is seen in the cockpit of P-38J-5 42-67291 in late 1944. He is officially credited with 4.5 aerial victories and 5 ground kills

following the delivery of the first P-51As to the 23rd FG. These were followed in early 1944 by Merlin-powered B- and D-model Mustangs, which at last made long-range raids into China feasible.

Returning to late 1943 and the Lightning, an F-5 photo-reconnaissance aircraft overflew the airfield at Shinchiku, on Formosa (Taiwan), on 24 November and revealed that it was packed with an estimated 200 Japanese aircraft.

The next day a force of fourteen B-25s, eight P-51As and eight P-38s made a low-level crossing over the straits between Suichuan and Shinchiku and hit the airfield in a surprise attack. Bob Schultz was only about 30 ft off the water when the legendary Lt Col 'Tex' Hill (15.25 kills in P-40s and P-51s), who was leading the raid as CO of the 23rd FG, called out that he had

**Hampton Boggs was the second-ranking ace of the 459th FS with nine kills. One of the first pilots transferred into the Lighting unit in October 1943 as a young lieutenant, he rose through the ranks until he was finally given command of the squadron in March 1945, having been promoted to major. Boggs was also one of the few pilots to score kills in three models of Lightning in the CBI, enjoying success with the H, J and L variants. Following the Japanese surrender in August 1945, Boggs visited several captured JAAF bases where he learned from Japanese Intelligence Officers that the P-38 was the most feared Allied fighter in Burma. Boggs later saw action in Korea, and having survived combat in two wars, was killed when his F-86F Sabre crashed in bad weather whilst attempting to land at Truax Field, Wisconsin, on 31 January 1953 (*Len Boyd*)**

**Maj Boggs' final score of aerial victories is seen painted on the nose of his P-38L-1 44-24240 *MELBA LOU IV*. CBI Lightnings were unique in retaining olive drab upper surfaces well into 1945 – long after Pacific P-38s had shed all traces of camouflage paint (*Sophus Larson*)**

spotted a Japanese transport aircraft coming into land at Shinchiku. Schultz reacted quickly and shot the transport down, before rejoining his flight.

Minutes later he saw the amazing sight of dozens of aircraft lined up on the field that he was scheduled to strafe once the B-25s had withdrawn. He sighted what he wistfully took to be a Ju 87 *Stuka* and promptly shot it down – an investigation into the identity of his second kill was instigated upon Schultz's return to base, and this eventually led to the conclusion that his victim had been a Ki-32 'Mary' light reconnaissance bomber.

From their vantage point as top cover for the bombers, the eight P-38 pilots were able to sweep in over the airfield ahead of the attacking formation and take their pick of the unsuspecting targets. Ten aircraft were destroyed in the air and many others on the ground, squadron CO Capt Sam Palmer accounting for one Zero, plus two other unidentified Japanese aircraft, to give him four kills in the P-38. At the time, his Command Headquarters gave him credit for another victory scored on 4 October 1943, but this was later reduced to a confirmed damage claim, thus denying him official status as an ace.

The 23rd FG's P-51A pilots also scored two victories, one of which was an 'Oscar II' claimed by 'Tex' Hill. All 30 USAAF aircraft returned safely from the long-range mission, which had been successfully completed thanks to them fully exploiting the crucial element of surprise

Lee Gregg continued on his inexorable march to 'acedom' on 12 December when he scored his fourth confirmed victory – a 'Tojo', plus another probably destroyed – during a mission to Hengyang. Lt Col George McMillan, who had recently been made CO of the 449th FS, was flying on the same mission and downed a second Ki-44 to follow on from his 'Nick' kill of two days before. McMillan had flown with the 3rd Pursuit Squadron of the AVG in 1941/42, scoring 4.5 victories in P-40Cs, before achieving more kills in P-38s with the 449th.

His next victory would be another Ki-45, but this time near Kanchang, on 10 February 1944 – on this same mission, Lt Keith Mahon also claimed a 'Nick' to open his P-38 account, which would eventually tally five air and five ground victories. McMillan would go on to score one more aerial kill (an 'Oscar' on 13 June 1944) to give him a final tally of

Texan Maxwell Glenn was the third-ranking ace within the 459th FS, and he scored all his kills (7.5 in total) between 11 March and 6 June 1944. It is likely that his final victim was 27-kill ace Capt Goichi Sumino of the 64th Sentai. Glenn survived the rigors of combat only to fall prey to illness in 1967 at the age of 50 (*INP*)

Maj Glenn's P-38J-10 *SLUGGO-IV* sports his impressive tally of air and ground kills in mid-1944 (*Paul McDaniel*)

8.5. Eleven days later he was killed when his P-38J-10LO (42-67633) was shot down by AA south-east of Pingsiang.

Two days after Mahon and McMillan had downed their 'Nicks', Lee Gregg got his fourth kill when the 449th ran into a mixed force of 'Tojos' and 'Oscars' north of Kanchow. During the course of the meleé, a Ki-44 fell to the guns of Gregg's P-38H, whilst he also reported damaging a Ki-43. A more general point of interest concerning this action is that equal numbers of both P-38Hs and P-51As were involved in the fighting, with the Mustang pilots claiming just one 'Oscar' (credited to 76th FS CO Capt John Stewart, who was already an ace on P-40s), while their Lightning counterparts downed six 'Tojos' and 'Oscars', and probably six others, for the loss of a single P-51. It seems that the P-38H definitely had the drop over the early Allison-engined Mustang in Chinese skies.

The 449th FS finally crowned its first ace on 4 March 1944 when Lee Gregg claimed an 'Oscar' destroyed and a second Nakajima fighter as damaged over Shihhweiyao, on the banks of the Yangtze River. During the same engagement fellow squadron stalwart Bob Schultz also got an 'Oscar' just minutes later, making him the unit's second ace.

## 'TWIN-TAILED DRAGONS'

The second unit to receive P-38s in the CBI was the 459th FS, who appropriately nicknamed themselves the 'Twin-tailed Dragons'. Activated in India on 1 September 1943, the unit was staffed by pilots and groundcrew sourced primarily from the 80th FG and 311th FBG – it also received a number of 'nugget' pilots directly from training units in the US. The 459th would be unique within the USAAF firstly due to it being formed outside of America, and secondly because it disestablished soon after VJ-Day, having never served in its parent country.

Training began with the P-38H – a type virtually unknown to maintenance crews and many of the pilots alike, who had been weaned on P-40s

P-38J-10 42-67626 *Miss-V* belonged to the 459th FS's ranking ace, Capt Walter Duke, who downed ten aircraft between 11 March and 23 May 1944 – six of them (all 'Oscars') in this very machine. He was also killed in this Lightning when a 20-strong patrol of 459th FS aircraft was ambushed by an overwhelming force of 64th Sentai Ki-43-IIs on 6 June 1944 over Myitche, Burma. Note the 'Twin-tailed Dragon' scheme adopted by the unit when it re-equipped with J-models in April 1944 (*via Ethell*)

– soon after the 459th's activation. New Lightnings were shipped from Madras to the unit's first operational base at Kurmitola, also in India, during November, the squadron undertaking its first combat mission as part of the 80th FG (then equipped exclusively with Warhawks) on the 20th of the month when a trio of P-38s escorted B-25s on a raid to Kalewa. The three Lightnings were led by Lt Hampton Boggs, an officer who had served with the 89th FS/80th FG on P-40s from late 1942 before transferring to the 459th on 25 October 1943. Not only would he later command the squadron, but he would also finish the war as its second ranking ace with nine kills.

On 1 December Boggs (P-38H-5 42-66994/'111') scored both his, and the squadron's, first confirmed victory when he shot down a 'Hamp' during a one-off mission to Rangoon. The morale of the squadron was extremely high during the period, in spite of the fact that they lost at least five P-38s in operational accidents during their first weeks in the frontline.

A crucial part of the unit's training in preparation for their wholesale commitment to combat over Burma was a visit to the RAF's legendary gunnery school at Armada Road (about 90 miles south-west of Calcutta), commencing on 9 February 1944. British instructors at the school were initially impressed with the interest shown by pilots in bettering their gunnery skills, and more than pleased with the rapid development of these techniques once the course had started. By the end of the month most pilots within the 459th had shown that they had the ability to destroy enemy aircraft both in the air and on the ground.

With its training complete, the unit moved to Chittagong, India (now Bangladesh), on 1 March, where it was placed under the control of the RAF's No 224 Group. The principal role of the 459th FS during the first half of 1944 would be to destroy Japanese aircraft both in the air and on the ground at their own bases. The airfields at Heho and Meiktila, in central Burma, would become favourite hunting grounds for the Lightning pilots, who regularly encountered the many aces of the crack 64th Sentai in their gaudily-painted Ki-43 'Oscars'.

The first important mission of this period was led by new squadron CO, Lt Col Verl Luehring, on 11 March, and saw a dozen Lightnings make a perfectly-timed assault on Aungban and Heho airstrips just as a number of Japanese fighters were taking off to intercept them. Luehring drew first blood when he shot down an 'Oscar' during his opening pass, whilst future aces Capts Maxwell Glenn (P-38H-5 42-66998/'125') and Willard Webb (P-38H-5 42-66982/'104') each accounted for a pair apiece. Eventual ranking ace of the 459th, Lt Walter Duke (P-38H-5 42-66980/'105'), got two Oscars as well, plus a third as a probable, and

Capt Duke is seen sitting in *Miss-V* at Chittagong in the spring of 1944. Like a number of pilots within the 459th FS, he had briefly flown frontline sorties with the P-40-equipped 89th FS in India, prior to transferring across to the newly-formed Lightning unit. Duke's official score of ten kills does not take into account information obtained by Hampton Boggs from Japanese Intelligence Officers after the war, the latter stating that he destroyed an additional three 'Oscar IIs' prior to being shot down and killed (*via Ethell*)

Lts Burdette Goodrich (P-38H-5 42-67001/'100') and Harry 'Lighthorse' Sealy (P-38H-5 42-66986/'126') each accounted for solitary Nakajima fighters – the latter ended his tour with 4.5 kills.

In addition to the 13 Japanese aircraft claimed in the air, a further nine were destroyed or damaged on the ground during the course of this mission. From that point on, the 459th flew countless strafing and dive-bombing sorties against key Japanese installations in the region, and although the fighter sweep would eventually become the most common type of mission detailed in pilots' logbooks, raids on Japanese airfields would continue until the fall of Myitkyina late in 1944.

Anisakan airfield was the next to feel the effects of a visit by the 'Twin-tailed Dragons' on 25 March. Hampton Boggs (P-38H-5 42-67013/'113') had led a flight of Lightnings on a morning sweep over Burma at 25,000 ft, but had failed to find any targets over the first few Japanese bases overflown. Finally, as the fighters closed on the airfield at Anisakan, he sighted a host of 'Oscars' in the process of landing. Boggs immediately led his P-38s down to tree-top height and effected a fast bounce. He single-handedly accounted for three Japanese fighters ('Oscars' that he misidentified as 'Hamps'), while Lts Duke (P-38H-5 42-66710/'102') and Smith shared a Ki-43 between them. Several other 'Oscars' were claimed in the air or on the ground by the diving Lightnings, who also lost two of their number to the Japanese.

April saw the 459th really come into its own as a attacking force in Burma, JAAF pilots fearing the P-38 to the point where they bestowed upon it mythical warrior qualities. Things only got worse for the Japanese with the arrival of the P-38J that same month, the newer version of the Lightning being not only faster than the H-model, but also boasting a greater range. This re-equipment coincided with the application of a

Lt Aaron 'Al' Bearden also 'made ace' during the ceaseless series of offensive patrols flown over Burma by the 459th FS in the spring of 1944, claiming five aerial victories (his scoreboard also denotes his 1.5 ground kills) before he collided with another P-38 and was captured on 3 September (*Len Boyd*)

Another 459th FS pilot to score five kills in early 1944 was Maj Willard J Webb, seen here loading rockets in-to 'Bazooka tubes' which were bolted onto his P-38J-10 in the field. Webb also later fought in the Korean War (*McDaniel*)

A quartet of 459th FS P-38Js make a low pass over their Nagaghuli base in the spring of 1944. From any angle, the Lightning made for an unmistakable sight in the skies over Burma (*IWM*)

gaudy green, yellow and red motif onto the booms of a number of the new P-38s, which gave the squadron's aircraft a dragon-like appearance!

Lt Boggs (P-38H-5 42-66995/'116') got the month off to a great start by becoming the unit's first ace on the 2nd – he and Maxwell Glenn (flying '125' again) each shot down an 'Oscar' during a sweep over Heho. Two other Japanese fighters were shot down and a further eight claimed as destroyed on the ground, but one P-38 was lost and its pilot captured, while a second was obliged to return to Chittagong on a single engine. On this occasion all the Lightnings returned home safely. In point of fact, no less than 26 459th Lightnings returned from combat missions with an engine out during the war, this experience making the pilots involved fully appreciative of the extra safety margin provided by the P-38's second engine.

Heho was visited once again on 17 April, and in a repeat of the Anisakan mission of the previous month, a number of 'Oscars' were caught in the landing pattern over the airfield. Lt Col Luehring led the nine P-38s on a devastating pass at tree-top level across the airstrip, downing seven 'Oscars' and destroying two more on the ground.

Amongst the band of 26 pilots who had the dubious distinction of logging combat time in a single-engined P-38 was Burdette Goodrich who, on 25 April, was part of a force that had been sent to raid Heho yet again. The early phase of the attack had gone well for him, as he had downed an 'Oscar' in the opening pass over the airfield. However, just as he began to pull P-38H-5 42-67009/'115' up from a second strafing run over the fighter dispersal, his ears were filled with a deafening din that sounded like a runaway machine gun. Seconds later he was alarmed to see that the manifold pressure in his right engine had drastically dropped, and a longing glance at the offending powerplant soon showed why – a large bulge had appeared atop the right engine cowl.

Goodrich immediately feathered the starboard Allison, having already opened the throttle wide on the left engine. Through a combination of sheer skill and lady luck, he managed to evade both the AA fire (which had knocked out his engine) over the airfield and an 'Oscar' that had come bearing down onto the tail of the crippled P-38. Capt Duke had also spotted Goodrich's predicament, and he too dove down from a higher altitude to cover the ailing P-38 while it raced for home on a single engine. Following his clearance of the surrounding Chin Hills, Goodrich could reduce manifold pressure to a more normal 35 inches, and the solitary engine performed satisfactorily until the fighter landed some 30 minutes later. Groundcrews back at Chittagong discovered soon after that the overworked left engine manifold had been discoloured to a bright orange following its exertions during the course of this sortie.

Earlier in that mission Duke (P-38J-10 42-67626) had managed to

claim his fifth fighter kill (an 'Oscar') to become only the second ace of the 459th. Aside from helping Goodrich extricate himself from this mission on a solitary engine, Duke (P-38H-5 42-66995/'116') had shared in a 'Tojo' kill with him just 48 hours before over Meiktila. Sadly, both pilots were lost in action during another attack on this airfield on 6 June 1944, Goodrich (P-38H-5 42-67001/'100') crashlanding into captivity soon after scoring his fifth, and last kill – he later died in a PoW camp on 1 January 1945. There was also hope at first that Duke (P-38J-10 42-67626/'2') had also been captured, but it later transpired that he had actually been killed in action.

As alluded to in the previous paragraph, the 6 June raid on Meiktila proved to be a disaster for the 459th FS, the unit falling into a trap set by the JAAF, who had become rather tired of the unit's raids on their airfields over the previous three months.

Some 20 P-38s had set out from Chittagong on the early-morning raid, the force being split into two groups of ten each, led by Lt Col Luehring and Capt Broadfoot respectively. Whilst flying over the western edge of the Burma Valley, the P-38s were jumped by an overwhelming force of 'Oscars' and were forced to fight their way out of the trap. One of the first pilots to free himself of Ki-43s was Capt Duke, who noticed that both Lts William Baumeister and Burdett Goodrich were missing from his group, so he turned back into the fray to try and find them.

Baumeister had actually seen Goodrich's P-38 mortally hit by fire from a Ki-43, and had stayed with him until he had crash-landed in the jungle below. He then turned back in the direction of Chittagong and managed

Wally Duke is watched by his groundcrew as he adds the final touches to the nose-art of *Miss-V* at Chittagong in late May 1944 (*Boyd*)

**459th FS ace Lt Burdette Goodrich scored all bar one of his 5.5 kills in this P-38H-5 (42-67001), nicknamed *Duffy*. His shared victory took the form of a 'Tojo', downed with the assistance of Wally Duke on 23 April 1944 – this was one of the few Ki-44 kills claimed in Burma. Like Duke, Goodrich was shot down on 6 June 1944 (in this very Lightning), and although he was made a PoW, he died in captivity on 1 January 1945 (*Boyd*)**

to return to base unscathed. Whilst this was going on, Duke's search for the two 'missing' P-38s had only led him into mortal danger, as a number of flights of 'Oscars' (and/or Zeros) had stayed above the fight looking for just such a lone target as that now presented to them by the 459th's leading ace. The Japanese fighters dived into the attack, but lost three of their number to other P-38s still in the area before Duke finally fell to their overwhelming weight of fire.

Hampton Boggs interviewed a number of Japanese Air Intelligence Officers in respect to this action in the weeks after the war had ended and was told the story from their side. He also ascertained that one of the Japanese lost during the fight was Goichi Sumino, a 25-kill ace with the 64th Sentai who was shot down during the course of this ambush when his 'Oscar' was struck in the cockpit by a burst from a 459th P-38.

## LAST VICTORIES IN THE CBI

The final kills of the war for the 449th FS were gained on 5 January 1945 by two P-38 pilots who became aces during the course of this mission. Capt Ralph Wire had scored three P-38 victories with the 49th FG in New Guinea in 1943, and he brought these with him to the CBI when he assumed command of the 449th in November 1944. Keith Mahon had scored his two kills earlier in his CBI tour, and had also destroyed five Japanese aircraft on the ground.

Nine 449th P-38Js had taken off from Kunming on the 5 January mission, bound for Samah Bay airfield on Hainan Island. Once over the target, they proceeded to make a number of gunnery passes on the near-deserted airstrip, destroying one 'Oscar' and damaging several others. Whilst in the process of carrying out their strafing runs, the P-38s were confronted by a number of Ki-43s who appeared over the airfield during their attack. The USAAF pilots were duly forced into a desperate defensive fight against the more numerous Japanese fighters, with Mahon, in particular, responding admirably to the unexpected challenge by downing a trio of 'Oscars' – not to be outdone, Wire shot down a pair of Ki-43s. Despite these successes, three of the nine P-38s were lost, although all the pilots were later recovered.

The 459th FS, meanwhile, had been forced to settle into the relatively unglamorous routine of strafing roads, bridges, oil storage plants and the like, and scored relatively few aerial victories after the great raids on the airfields between March and June 1944 ceased. Fittingly, the unit's 82nd, and last, victory fell to Hampton Boggs (P-38L-1 44-24240/'6') whilst he was escorting B-24s on a bombing raid to Rangoon on 11 February 1945. He had scored the unit's first victory back on 1 December 1943, and had gone on to become its first ace.

On the occasion of this final kill, Boggs had noticed a type of Japanese aircraft that he had never seen before attempting to engage the bombers just as they were leaving the target. He led his flight down to intercept the lone attacker, and was amazed when the Ki-61 'Tony' (as it was now identified) simply flew on totally oblivious to the closing Lightnings. Boggs coolly flew up behind the enemy fighter and fired away when he drew within range, the 'Tony' blowing up literally seconds after the first burst struck home. It was a prosaic end to the spectacular career of the CBI Lightnings.

# BONG AND McGUIRE

## RICHARD IRA BONG

T here are three indispensable qualities that make up an ace fighter pilot – skill, determination and luck. Dick Bong was the ranking American ace of all time, and he possessed the first two qualities in copious amounts. However, his extensive success in aerial combat was due primarily to luck. On the face of it this may seem an unfair judgement to make in respect to America's 'ace of aces', but a quick glance at the number of missions he flew in which he encountered the enemy reveals just how lucky he was – particularly when the ratio of sorties to victories is compared with other leading pilots in the Pacific/CBI theatre.

Bong's luck also saw him through the operational practices of his old 9th FS, who would schedule pilots for combat sorties on alternate days. His squadron-mates were constantly amazed at how he would often run into Japanese opposition on the days that he flew, whilst no enemy activity would be encountered on the days that he was stood down.

For part of his first tour he flew on even-numbered days, and a brief look at his victory list shows that he confirmed an 'Oscar' on 12 June 1943 for his 11th victory, whilst his next claims were on 26 July when he enjoyed his highest scoring day of his career with two 'Oscars' and two 'Tonys' destroyed. On his next scheduled mission flown two days later, the 9th ran into a gaggle of interceptors and Bong got another 'Oscar' for his 16th victory.

Dick Bong was something of a curiosity to other fighter pilots in New Guinea. Texan Jay Robbins met him around the time that both men came to New Guinea in the latter part of 1942. He later stated that he would never have guessed that anyone with such a mild personality could have become any sort of fighter ace, much less the ranking ace of the war. Others who met Bong were impressed by the self-effacing informality of the young pilot, his shy smile and friendly eyes being more suggestive of a member of the 'fishing hole' fraternity common to his native north-western Wisconsin, rather than the deadly skies of the wartime Pacific.

But there was a 'Jekyll and Hyde' type transformation that took place

Capt Dick Bong is seen sitting in the cockpit of P-38J-15 42-103993 on 30 March 1944 whilst part of the Fifth Fighter Command HQ flight. His score then stood at 24, just two short of Eddie Rickenbacker's record of 26 kills, which dated from World War 1. Within a fortnight of this photo being taken, now Maj Dick Bong had become the ranking US ace of all time – a position he has retained to this day (*USAF Museum*)

On 12 December 1944 Maj Bong was awarded the Medal of Honor by Gen Douglas MacArthur (seen here in the raincoat) at Tacloban airfield, on Leyte (*Wagenknecht via Krane*)

The detail markings on the nose of P-38J-15 42-103993 *Marge*, seen at Cape Gloucester in March 1944. Deep contrast on the original negative of this shot led many historians to believe that the nose marking was red while the anti-glare panel was black. In point of fact, Bong did use red as his ID colour, but had an olive drab anti-glare panel *Marge* was also applied in red, with a white outline

in Bong when airborne in the cockpit of his P-38. His flying comrades were taken aback when he would call out over the radio in the rawest language possible that he had just claimed another kill. Bomber crewmen stated that his P-38 was always visible in the midst of even the hottest air battles, and a number of them who later met Bong on the ground became his most loyal devotees when he praised their sacrifice when compared with his own as a mere fighter pilot.

Although Bong did make a transformation when aloft from retiring youth to daring pilot, he was not one to throw caution to the wind. He was careful in planning his flights, and used the most logical approach to the science of flying. The P-38 that he flew became a part of his consciousness, and he had a greater affection for the Lockheed fighter than any other aircraft he piloted during his career – including the tractable P-51D, which most pilots agree was perhaps the best wartime American fighter from a flying point of view.

After gaining his 40th aerial victory on 17 December 1944, Dick Bong was taken out of combat for the third time and sent home. He married his sweetheart, Marge Vattendahl, in February of 1945, and on 23 June assumed duties as Chief of Flight Operations for the USAAF at the Lockheed plant in Burbank, California. Sadly, he was killed when a new P-80 jet that he was testing crashed soon after take-off on 6 August 1945.

Bong had left Superior State Teacher's College in 1941 to enter the USAAF Flying Cadet programme, and when he won his wings he was initially assigned instructor's duties. After his second tour had ended in April 1944, he was again sent back to the US to fill an instructor's post, before he finally worked his way back into combat as a Gunnery Training Officer with Fifth Fighter Command. It is easy to speculate that America's top ace, and holder of the Medal of Honor, would likely have found his way into a teaching position had he lived to retire from the USAAF.

Although of poor quality, this shot nevertheless shows Bong's scoreboard as applied to P-38L-1 44-23964 of the 8th FS. This aircraft was lost along with its pilot, Capt John Davis, on 28 November 1944 when it crashed during an aborted take-off

# THOMAS BUCHANAN MCGUIRE

As Bong's chief rival for the position of 'ace of aces', Tom McGuire was also the recipient of America's highest award for bravery, the Medal of Honor, and he too had ample amounts of luck on his side. His special gift, however, was determination, laced with a unique fearlessness. McGuire became a fighter pilot in February 1942, and was sent on a tour of duty with the 56th PS/54th PG to the Aleutians in P-39Fs, before he managed to obtain a transfer firstly to the 9th FS/49th FG and then the 431st FS, of the newly-formed 475th FG, in July 1943.

Some of McGuire's old flying comrades at the 56th PS were surprised at his phenomenal successes during the 431st's opening combats, for although they had considered him a fair pilot, his ability seemed little better than average, which hardly made him a candidate for major ace status. They also found his growing reputation as an unstoppable talker when airborne hard to fathom, since he had been known as a quiet pilot before his assignment to the New Guinea front.

The reasons behind these dramatic changes in skill level and personality lie in the emergence of an aggressive spirit that was displayed more and more when contact with the Japanese became commonplace. This was perhaps best shown after McGuire was badly wounded in the wrist and buttocks and forced to bail out during a big air battle over Oro Bay on 17 October 1943. Prior to taking to his parachute he had shot down three Zeros to take his tally to 13 victories, and he immediately pressed the crew of the patrol boat that picked him up after 45 minutes in shark-infested waters to confirm his kills for the day! Soon after leaving his hospital bed after a number of weeks convalescing, McGuire waded into another batch of Japanese aircraft on Boxing Day 1943 over Cape Gloucester, quickly downing three 'Vals'.

This rare shot of a smiling Maj Tom McGuire shows him devoid of his distinctively battered service hat, which was a permanent fixture atop his head when the 'Iron Major' was not flying

Many apocryphal stories are told about the audacity of Tom McGuire in the cockpit of his P-38, and one of his favourite post-sortie antics was also performed by Dick Bong. The art of the hair-raising landing was perfected by both aces, and would usually involve a half-loop over the runway during final approach, followed by the extension of the landing gear while upside down, before gently righting the big fighter and gliding in for a perfect landing before the rest of his flight could catch up!

It was perhaps McGuire's extreme courage that finally brought about his undoing on 7 January 1945 over the island of Negros, in the Philippines. Knowing he was due to return back to the US the following month tour-expired, he was anxious to pass Bong's mark of 40 kills. Any opportunity to take on the enemy was therefore jumped at, but an endless series of fighter sweeps flown since McGuire had achieved his 38th kill on Boxing Day had failed to find any sign of the Japanese. The major decided to try his luck again on the 7th, holding an impromptu brief late in the evening of the 6th. He would take three other seasoned 431st FS pilots with him on a sweep to Mindoro, departing at dawn.

Sunrise at Dulag's Marston airstrip, on Leyte, the following day found a mixed quartet of J-15s and L-1s that comprised 'Daddy Flight' already running up, with Tom McGuire completing his cockpit checks in 44-24845/'112' by torch light. With everything in order, the major gave the signal to taxy out, and within minutes the Lightnings were airborne and forming up around their leader. Heading north-west towards Negros Island, the flight initially levelled out at 10,000 ft, but the sight of an approaching tropical weather front forced them down to 6000 ft in an attempt to pierce the storm.

On the other side of the weather,

WO Akira Sugimoto of the 54th Sentai was fruitlessly searching for a suspected American convoy in his Ki-43, having been given strict orders to bomb it if it was found. He too was finding the weather worsening, and was on the verge of returning home to Negros Island. Not too many miles away, Sgt Mizunori Fukuda was commencing his final descent into Manalpa strip, also on Negros, in a near-new 71st Sentai Ki-84, having also been scouting for the convoy.

In the meantime 'Daddy Flight' had successfully penetrated the storm and now found itself over Fabrica airstrip, on the eastern side of Negros. However, none of the 15 fighters sighted on the dispersal made any attempt to take-off, and with strict orders not to strafe the target, McGuire pushed on to the airfields on the western side of the island. Some 15 miles short of Manalpa, the Lightnings spotted Sugimoto, who was returning to base on a near collision course with the four USAAF

**Tom McGuire poses with his groundcrewmen, Richard Van Der Geest (left) and Frank Kish (right), in front of P-38J-15 *PUDGY III* in May 1944. This aircraft survived over six months in the frontline before being replaced by . . .**

**. . . *PUDGY IV* when the 431st FS received L-1s. Like Bong's *Marge*, this P-38 was also the victim of postwar misinterpretation concerning its markings. It *did not* sport a yellow kill tally box until after McGuire had arrived in the Philippines, and the 431st FS's 'demon' *did not* appear on the booms of the unit's P-38s until January 1945**

fighters. The Ki-43 pilot spotted the quartet just as he passed some 500 ft beneath them, and he immediately opened the throttle wide on his fighter and commenced a defensive turn into the enemy. McGuire quickly ordered his flight to surround the lone 'Oscar' by forming a Lufbery circle, but also told them to keep their auxiliary fuel tanks in place, rather than jettisoning them as was standard operational procedure when the enemy was engaged.

Sugimoto realised that he best form of defence was to try and turn inside the big Lightnings and single out one as a target. His 'Oscar' was

ideally suited to the task, and he quickly lined up on Capt Ed Weaver, having earlier been shot off the tail of Lt Doug Thropp's P-38. McGuire, sensing the urgency in Weaver's voice as he called for help over the radio, attempted a tight turn with low speed and altitude in order to get on the tail of the persistent Sugimoto, who was proving anything but an easy kill. However, the added weight of the auxiliary tanks proved too much for the straining Lightning, and the silver fighter shuddered on the edge of a massive stall.

McGuire struggled to increase the power in an effort to 'dig' the Lightning out of the precarious position it was now in, but with marginal flying speed 'on the clock', the fighter snap-rolled into a spin at a mere 200 ft above the ground and dropped like a stone inverted into the jungle below. Sgt Fukuda had seen the 'Oscar' bravely take on the quartet of P-38s, and quickly cycled away his landing gear and raced into the fray in an effort to even the odds. As he arrived at great speed he saw McGuire's Lightning explode as it hit the ground, and then proceeded to shoot down Maj Jack Rittmayer in a single pass before fleeing the scene. Fukuda was forced to crash land at Manapla, his 'Frank' having been hit 23 times by fire from Ed Weaver's P-38

Fukuda, meanwhile, had used the element of confusion generated by McGuire's crash to make his exit, although his badly shot up Ki-43 struggled to reach the safety of a nearby cloud bank. The mountains between him and Manapla now loomed ahead, and he realised that he would have to set his 'Oscar' down as it was in no shape to climb over them. Spotting a flat clearing, Fukuda executed a safe wheels up landing, but as he attempted to extricate himself from his steaming fighter, a band of Filippino guerillas loomed out of the undergrowth and shot him six times in the chest, before disappearing back into the jungle.

The two surviving P-38 pilots had by this stage returned to Dulag, where news of the demise of the 'Iron Major' was greeted with incredulity by his contemporaries in the 475th FG.

Years later McGuire Air Force Base, near Fort Dix in New Jersey, was so named as a permanent tribute to the valiant Medal of Honor winner who grew up in that state.

The four great aces of the 475th FG are seen together in mid-1944 at Biak. They are, from left to right, Capt Frank Lent (11 victories), Maj Tom McGuire (38 victories) Col Charles MacDonald (27 victories) and Lt Col John Loisel (11 victories). Only the latter two pilots would survive to see VJ-Day (*Krane Collection*)

# APPENDICES

## P-38 LIGHTNING ACES OF WORLD WAR 2
### IN THE PACIFIC AND CBI

### Fifth Air Force

| | |
|---|---|
| Richard Bong | 40 |
| Thomas McGuire | 38 |
| Charles MacDonald | 27 |
| Gerald Johnson | 22 |
| Jay Robbins | 22 |
| Thomas Lynch | 17 (20) |
| Edward Cragg | 15 |
| Cyril Homer | 15 |
| Daniel Roberts | 13 (15) |
| Kenneth Ladd | 12 |
| James Watkins | 11 (12) |
| Francis Lent | 11 |
| John Loisel | 11 |
| Cornelius Smith | 11 |
| Kenneth Sparks | 11 |
| William Giroux | 10 |
| Paul Stanch | 10 |
| Elliot Summer | 10 |
| George Welch | 9 |
| Fredric Champlin | 9 |
| Perry Dahl | 9 |
| Joseph Forster | 9 |
| Allen Hill | 9 |
| Joel Paris | 9 |
| Meryl Smith | 9 |
| Richard West | 8 (14) |
| Fernley Damstrom | 8 |
| Frederick Harris | 8 |
| Kenneth Hart | 8 |
| John Jones | 8 |
| John O'Neill | 8 |
| Robert Ashenbrener | 7 (10) |
| Burnell Adams | 7 (8) |
| Zach Dean | 7 |
| John Dunaway | 7 |
| Vincent Elliott | 7 |
| Jack Fisk | 7 |
| Warren Lewis | 7 |
| John Purdy | 7 |
| Richard Smith | 7 |
| Calvin Wire | 7 |
| Verl Jett | 6 (7) |

| | |
|---|---|
| Stanley Andrews | 6 |
| Edward Czarnecki | 6 |
| Edwin Degraffenreid | 6 |
| William Drier | 6 |
| Hoyt Eason | 6 |
| Charles Gallup | 6 |
| Billy Gresham | 6 |
| James Ince | 6 |
| John Lane | 6 |
| Paul Lucas | 6 |
| Paul Murphey | 6 |
| John Pietz | 6 |
| John Smith | 6 |
| Harry Brown | 5 (7) |
| Wallace Jordan | 5 (6) |
| Ralph Wandrey | 5 (6) |
| Arthur Wenige | 5 (6) |
| Robert Adams | 5 |
| Ernest Ambort | 5 |
| Nial Castle | 5 |
| Vivian Cloud | 5 |
| Harry Condon | 5 |
| Warren Curton | 5 |
| Cheatham Gupton | 5 |
| Charles King | 5 |
| Marion Kirby | 5 |
| Lowell Lutton | 5 |
| Jack Mankin | 5 |
| Milden Mathre | 5 |
| Franklin Monk | 5 |
| Paul Morriss | 5 |
| Jennings Myers | 5 |
| Charles Ray | 5 |
| John Tilley | 5 |
| Marion Felts | 4 (5) |
| Grover Gholson | 4 (5) |
| Curran Jones | 4 (5) |
| Joseph McKeon | 4 (5) |
| Kenneth Pool | 4 (5) |
| Richard Suehr | 4 (5) |
| Charles O'Sullivan | 4 (6) |
| Frederick Dick | 3 (5) |
| Nelson Flack | 3 (5) |

### Thirteenth Air Force

| | |
|---|---|
| Bill Harris | 16 |
| Robert Westbrook | 13 (20) |
| Murray Shubin | 11 |
| Cotesworth Head | 8 (14) |
| Henry Meigs, II | 6 |
| Thomas Walker | 6 |
| Rex Barber | 5 |
| Truman Barnes | 5 |
| George Chandler | 5 |
| Besby Holmes | 5 |
| Thomas Lanphier | 5* |

### CBI

| | |
|---|---|
| Walter Duke | 10 |
| Hampton Boggs | 9 |
| Maxwell Glenn | 7.5 |
| Lee Gregg | 7 |
| Burdette Goodrich | 5.5 |
| Aaron Bearden | 5 |
| Keith Mahon | 5 |
| Robert Schultz | 5 |
| Willard Webb | 5 |
| Harry Sealy | 4.5** |

() Final score in brackets
* Traditional inclusion since Lanphier's
score was officially reduced to 4.5
** Plus six on the ground

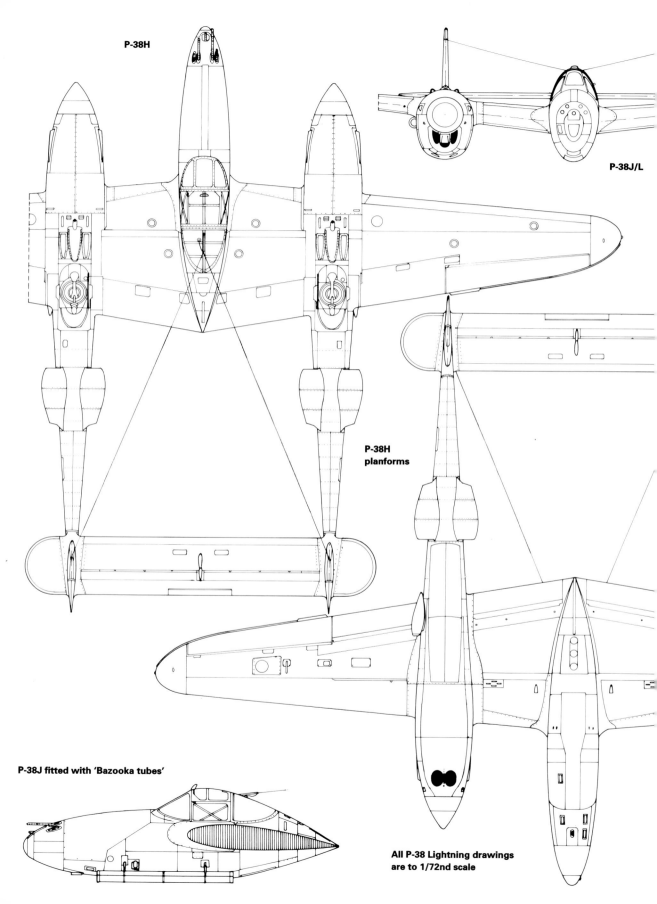

P-38H

P-38J/L

P-38H
planforms

P-38J fitted with 'Bazooka tubes'

All P-38 Lightning drawings
are to 1/72nd scale

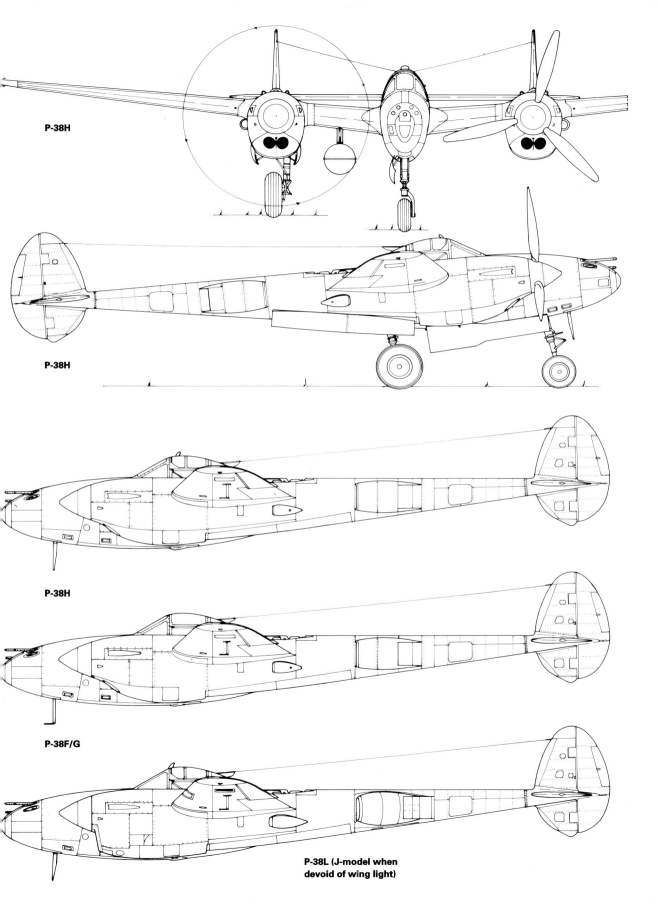

**P-38H**

**P-38H**

**P-38H**

**P-38F/G**

**P-38L (J-model when devoid of wing light)**

## 1

**P-38F-5 42-12644/ *Thumper* of Lt John 'Shady' Lane, 39th FS/35th FG, Port Moresby, December 1942**

Lane dubbed this Lightning *Thumper*, but apparently the only application of artwork on the port side was a small rendition of a reclining bathing beauty. Dick Bong scored his first two confirmed victories in this P-38 when he was scrambled on 27 December 1942 – following this sortie Lane jokingly professed that he would never again allow his aircraft to be flown in combat by anyone but himself. He got his first confirmed victory in P-38F-5 42-12638 some four days later, and went on to claim a Zeke destroyed and a second unidentified fighter as a probable in 42-12644 on 18 July 1943 over Lae.

## 2

**P-38F-5 42-12654/ *Regina I* of Lt Paul Stanch, 39th FS/35th FG, Port Moresby, January 1943**

Double ace Stanch scored his first victories (a pair of Zeros on 3 March 1943) in this Lightning. These kills came as a great relief to his 39th FS CO, Maj George Prentice, who was already in the sights of more than one Japanese fighter when Stanch came to the aid of his leader and shot the offending fighters off his tail 70 miles east of Lae.

## 3

**P-38G-13 43-2187/ *Diablo* of Lt Rex Barber, 339th FS/347th FG, Guadalcanal, April 1943**

There is some conjecture as to the appearance of this machine in the aftermath of the famous Yamamoto mission of 18 April 1943 in which its pilot played a crucial part – it was Barber's assigned P-38, but was unserviceable on this fateful day, forcing him to fly 43-2204 (see next profile). Photos of the subsequent award ceremony that took place to honour the participants of Operation *Dillinger* show the Lightning with seven kill marks on its nose, but its pilot has subsequently stated that the P-38 was decorated with only three victory flags, plus the silhouette of a ship that Barber had earlier been credited with sinking. The right side of 'White 110' had a small red Satan's head figure and the name *Diablo* in script painted on it.

## 4

**P-38G-13 43-2204/ *Miss Virginia* of Lts Rex Barber and Bob Petit, 339th FS/347th FG, Guadalcanal, April 1943**

This was the aircraft flown by Rex Barber during the Yamamoto mission, having been borrowed from its regular pilot, Lt Bob Petit. The ship silhouette on the nose signifies a sinking made by the latter on 29 March, whilst the two victory flags belong to Barber, who downed a pair of Zeros in this fighter off Cape Esperance on 7 April.

## 5

**P-38H-1 42-66528/ *PRINCESS PAT* of Lt Bob Adams, 80th FS/8th FG, Port Moresby, July 1943**

This Lightning was used by Adams to claim a Zeke kill (and a probable) on 21 July 1943 near Bogadjim, and was one of five different P-38s employed by the ace to score as many victories. He became obsessed with killing the enemy at all cost after witnessing the strafing of squadron-mate Lt Murtha McCarthy by a Japanese fighter pilot while he hung helplessly in his parachute – Adams had arrived on the scene too late to save his comrade. From this day forth he flew without regard for his own safety until he was finally killed in action over Wewak on 2 September 1943. Adams' final two confirmed victories (which gave him ace status) were an 'Oscar' and a 'Nick', claimed again over Wewak three days prior to his death.

## 6

**P-38H-1 42-66532 of Maj Tom Lynch, CO of the 39th FS/35th FG, Tsili Tsili, September 1943**

Lynch flew 'White 10' almost exclusively between March and September 1943, although he only scored kills in it during his last month with the 39th – he returned home on leave on 20 September, being relieved by five-kill ace, Capt C W King. Lynch scored five victories in this P-38, a tally which included one of the first Ki-48 'Lily' bombers to fall to Fifth Fighter Command, downed on 4 September 1943 over the Huon Gulf.

## 7

**P-38H-5 42-66845 of Lt Grover Fanning, 9th FS/49th FG, Dobodura, October 1943**

Fanning shared this Lightning with Lt Harry Lidstrom during the autumn months of 1943. He had earlier scored the 49th FG's 200th confirmed victory when he shot down a 'Betty' and damaged a second Mitsubishi bomber, plus claimed an 'Oscar' as a probable, in his first real combat on 12 April 1943 south of Port Moresby. Fanning claimed his ninth, and last, kill (a 'Tony') over Oro Bay on 17 October 1943 almost certainly in this P-38. His squadron-mate Lidstrom had been lost in an operational accident just 24 hours earlier, and Fanning added his name to the side of 'White 97' as a sign of respect for his fallen comrade.

## 8

**P-38H-1 42-66573 of Capts Fred Harris and Campbell Wilson, 432nd FS/475th FG, Dobodura, October 1943**

Harris downed two Zekes and a 'Betty' during the invasion of Finschhafen on 22 September 1943, although he wasn't flying this fighter at the time – he used P-38H-5 42-66869. Indeed, none of his eight kills were scored whilst flying this, his assigned Lightning. He was killed in a flying accident near Buma Bay on 31 October 1943 whilst performing an air test in P-38H-1 42-66595.

## 9

**P-38H-5 42-66856/ *Regina Coeli* of Capt Joe McKeon, 433rd FS/475th FG, Dobodura, October 1943**

McKeon claimed two kills in this P-38, a 'Hamp' on 24 September over Finschhafen and a 'Val' on 15 October over Oro Bay – the second score made him an ace. *Regina Coeli* is Latin for 'queen of the sky', and well reflects the affection McKeon had for his P-38. Having completed 144 missions by January 1944, McKeon returned to the US and spent six months instructing before being posted to the 77th FS/20th FG in England. He claimed one more kill whilst flying a P-51D-5 in August 1944, but was made a PoW some two months later following a collision with another Mustang over Germany.

## 10

**P-38 (serial unknown) of Capt Gerald Johnson, CO of the**

**9th FS/49th FG, Dobodura, November 1943**

On 2 November 1943 Johnson scored his eighth and ninth kills over Rabaul in this P-38 during the famed low-level mission that became known as 'Bloody Tuesday' – he also shot down a RAAF Wirraway fighter-bomber by mistake in this Lightning on the 15th of this month! The two diagonal stripes on the rudder of the fighter denote that it is flown by the CO of the 9th FS.

## 11

**P-38H-1 42-66568/*Impossible Ince* of Lt James C Ince, 432nd FS/475th FG, Dobodura, November 1943**

'Impossible Jim' Ince gained the last two (Zekes) of his six victories in this suitably decorated P-38 on 9 and 16 November 1943. Prior to joining the 432nd, he had scored two kills with the 80th FS flying F- and G-model Lightnings.

## 12

**P-38H-5 42-66752 of Capt Daniel T Roberts, CO of the 433rd FS/475th FG, Dobodura, November 1943**

Known as the 'quiet ace', Danny Roberts scored three kills (all Zekes) and one probable (again a Zeke) in this P-38 in the second half of October. His final score is now considered to have been 15 if the Zeke he claimed on 2 November 1943 (in this very Lightning) is allowed. Roberts was killed when his P-38 (42-66834) was in collision with another Lightning over Alexishafen on 9 November 1943.

## 13

**P-38H-1 42-66506/*PORKY II* of Maj Edward 'Porky' Cragg, CO of the 80th FS/8th FG, Finschhafen, December 1943**

No less than nine of Cragg's fifteen victories were scored in *PORKY II*, and all of these were fighters. On 22 December 1943 he was involved in a harrowing incident when his P-38 inadvertently shredded the parachute of a descending Ki-61 'Tony' pilot whose aircraft he had just shot down over Wewak. Four days later Cragg was lost in this P-38 after gaining his final victory (a 'Tojo') over Cape Gloucester.

## 14

**P-38H-5 42-66817/*PUDGY* of Capt Tom McGuire, 431st FS/475th FG, Dobodura, December 1943**

This H-5 was McGuire's second P-38, his first *PUDGY* (H-1 42-66592) having been written off following damage inflicted by enemy cannon fire during a dogfight near Wewak on 29 August 1943 – its pilot claimed a Zeke and a 'Tony' destroyed in return. This machine lasted until it was replaced by a new J-model in late January 1944, McGuire having by that stage raised his score to 16 confirmed (few of these were claimed in this Lightning, however), 2 probables and 2 damaged.

## 15

**P-38H-1 42-66666/*MISS FRU-FRU II* of Lt Vincent T Elliott, 431st FS/475th FG, Dobodura, December 1943**

This distinctively-marked P-38 was Elliott's assigned mount during the autumn of 1943, and he managed to claim a Zeke and a 'Hamp' in it during the high altitude raid on Rabaul on 23 October. With the subsequent confirmation of these victories, Elliott became the first P-38 pilot to score five kills over Rabaul.

## 16

**P-38J-10 42-67590/*BETTY* of Capt Jay T Robbins, CO of the**

**80th FS/8th FG, Finschhafen, late December 1943**

One of the first J-models to arrive in-theatre, this machine is unlikely to have been used by Robbins to score any of his kills, as from the New Year through to the end of March, the 80th saw little action. As CO, Robbins had the spinners on his fighter decorated in non-standard red, white and blue colours perhaps as an aid to identification when flying in formation.

## 17

**P-38H-1 42-66682/*SCREAMIN' KID* of Capt John Loisel, CO of the 432nd FS/475th FG, Dobodura, January 1944**

This fighter was by Loisel on and off until late January 1944, when the first J-models arrived in the Solomons. He definitely scored two Zeke kills in it on 15 October 1943 over Oro Bay, and it is likely that two other Mitsubishi fighters fell to its guns in December and January. On average, a P-38 could expect to survive less than six months with a Fifth Air Force unit, but *SCREAMIN' KID* somehow toughed it out for eight.

## 18

**P-38H-1 42-66504/*SKIDOO"* of Lt Perry Dahl, 432nd FS/475 FG, Dobodura, January 1944**

'Pee Wee' Dahl claimed his premier victory (a Zeke) during his very first encounter with the enemy on 9 November 1943 whilst flying this machine over Alexishafen airfield. His third kill (another Zeke), claimed in the Wewak area on 23 January 1944, was probably scored in this machine as well - it certainly carried Dahl's tally beneath its cockpit. Like John Loisel's mount, this P-38H-1 enjoyed a long service life in the frontline.

## 19

**P-38J-10 42-67898/*HILL'S ANGELS*/*Millie* of Lt Allen Hill, 80th FS/8th FG, Finschhafen, January 1944**

It is extremely likely that 'Ailing Allen' Hill scored his sixth kill (a 'Tony') over Wewak in this P-38 on 19 January 1944. Nose-art and nicknames were usually applied on the right side of the gun bay on Pacific P-38s by the aircraft's groundcrewmen.

## 20

**P-38J-5 42-67147/*Black Market Babe* of Lt Billy Gresham, 432nd FS/475th FG, Dobodura, January 1944**

Gresham is likely to have used this fighter to score his sixth, and last, victory (a Zeke) on 18 January 1944 over Wewak - his 'Oscar' probable of 31 March near Hollandia may have also been achieved in *'Babe*. Gresham was killed when his parachute streamed after he had bailed out of a mechanically-stricken P-38L-1LO (44-23958) near Biak on 2 October 1944.

## 21

**P-38J-5 42-6713/*SCREWY LOUIE* of Lt Louis Schriber, 80th FS/8th FG, Finschhafen, January 1944**

It is highly probable that Schriber scored his first confirmed victory (a 'Tony') over Wewak on 18 January 1944 in this P-38 - the reversed victory flags on his scoreboard in this profile denote his numerous probable kills claimed in 1943.

## 22

**P-38J-10 42-67580/*CORKY III* of Capt Cornelius 'Corky' Smith, 80th FS/8th FG, Finschhafen, February 1944**

It is probable that Smith used this P-38 to down a pair of Zekes over Wewak on the morning of 18 January 1944. He flew

CORKY III until it was replaced by his last P-38 – a J-15 – sometime in late March 1944.

## 23

### P-38J-5 42-67145/SWEET SUE of Lt Paul Murphey, 80th FS/8th FG, Nadzab, March 1944

There is no record that Murphey claimed any kills in this specific Lightning, although according to his logbook, only one of his six victims fell to the guns of a J-5 – a 'Tony' over Wewak on 22 December 1943. 80th FS maintenance records show that SWEET SUE was neither damaged or lost whilst with the unit, so it is highly likely that Murphey flew this P-38 until it was replaced in the spring of 1944 by a J-15.

## 24

### P-38J-15 42-103984/ "SAN ANTONIO ROSE" of Lt 'C B' Ray, 80th FS/8th FG, Nadzab, March 1944

Ray scored at least two of his victories (a 'Tony' on 30 March and an 'Oscar' four days later, both off Hollandia) while flying this P-38. He went on to claim one of the last 80th FS victories of the war on 29 December 1944 when he got a 'Dinah' over Mindoro Island, followed by a Zeke on a patrol flown later in the day over a convoy off the same island – he made ace with these kills.

## 25

### P-38J-15 42-103993/Marge of Capt Dick Bong, Fifth Fighter Command, Cape Gloucester, March 1944

Bong scored victories over a 'Tony' at Cape Hoskins, New Britain (15 February) and two 'Sallys' near Tadji (3 March), plus a probable 'Oscar' of the 77th Sentai, and a second Ki-43 damaged (5 March), all in Marge. This fighter was lost on 24 March 1944 during a weather reconnaissance flight, its pilot on this occasion, Capt Tom Malone, managing to parachute to safety.

## 26

### P-38J-15 42-104004 of Gen Paul Wurtsmith, Fifth Fighter Command, Gusap, March 1944

Lt Col Tom Lynch used this P-38 during the time that he and Bong flew together during the first months of 1944, although he was flying J-15 42-103987 when he was shot down by AA while strafing Japanese ships off Tadji on 9 March 1944. It is likely that Gen Wurtsmith offered his personal aircraft for Lynch's use in anticipation of the latter breaking the Rickenbacker record.

## 27

### P-38J-15 42-104032/T.RIGOR MORTIS III of Lt Frank Lent, 431st FS/475th FG, Nadzab, March 1944

Lent claimed his final victories (two Zekes) over Hollandia on 31 March 1944, which was around the same time as he began flying this garish J-15. Records exist of this P-38 being used after its original pilot had left the squadron. Lent was killed in a flying accident on 1 December 1944 when his F-6D Mustang (44-14621) crashed off Lae.

## 28

### P-38J-15 (serial unknown/CORKY IV/JAWONA) of Capt Cornelius 'Corky' Smith, 80th FS/8th FG, Nadzab, April 1944

Smith gained his 11th, and final, victory (an 'Oscar') over

Hollandia on 12 April 1944, and was rotated home the following month after completing 169 missions. As his last P-38, Smith's CORKY IV/JAWONA is finished in a scheme indicative of the colours and markings worn by the 80th FS from spring 1944 until war's end. Green had always been the squadron's identification colour within the 8th FG, and Smith had ensured that his personal markings (including the rudder stripes, which identified him as an old veteran to newer pilots) were applied in a compatible shade.

## 29

### P-38J-15 42-103988/JANDINA III of Capt Jay T Robbins, CO of the 80th FS/8th FG, Nadzab, April 1944

Robbins scored some, if not all, of his five Hollandia victories in this J-15 between 30 March and 12 April. JANDINA III was written off soon after in a crash-landing near Saidor after Robbins had experienced hydraulic problems in flight that prevented him from extending the nose gear.

## 30

### P-38J-15 42-104012/DOWN BEAT of Maj Dick Bong, Fifth Fighter Command, Nadzab, April 1944

80th FS legend (and Frank Olynyk's Stars & Bars) suggests that Bong used this J-15 from the unit to break the mythical Rickenbacker record of 26 aircraft and balloons shot down, but other sources state that he was flying his own P-38 on the mission in question (12 April 1944) to Hollandia, when he downed three 'Oscars' to take his score to 28.

## 31

### P-38J-15 (serial unknown) UNCLE CY'S Angel of Lt Cy Homer, 80th FS/8th FG, Nadzab, April 1944

It is believed that Homer used this P-38 to destroy two 'Tonys' and two 'Oscars' in a dogfight over Hollandia on 3 April 1944.

## 32

### P-38J-10 42-67626/Miss-V of Capt Walter F Duke, 459th FS/80th FG, Chittagong, May 1944

As the leading P-38 ace in the CBI, Duke used this distinctively-marked Lightning to gain six of his ten victories. Remarkably, 9.5 of the kills he scored in this fighter were 'Oscars' (he shared a 'Tojo' with fellow 459th FS ace Burdette Goodrich over Meiktila airfield on 23 April 1944), and it was almost certainly a Ki-43 that finally shot him down on 6 June 1944 – he was again flying Miss-V on this fateful occasion

## 33

### P-38J-15 (serial unknown/PUDGY III) of Maj Tom McGuire, CO of the 431st FS/475th FG, Hollandia, May 1944

This machine was McGuire's mount during the first half of 1944, and it is believed that he scored at least two victories in it – an 'Oscar' on 17 May over Noemfoor Island, and a 'Tojo' 48 hours later near Manokwari, New Guinea. Like an number of the aces' machines featured in this volume, PUDGY III enjoyed an unusually long service life of around six months (late January through to early July 1944). McGuire was severe in the use of his P-38s, and used up his next two fighters between July and December 1944.

## 34

### P-38J-15 42-104024/PUTT PUTT MARU of Col Charles

**MacDonald, CO of the 475th FG, Lingayen , June 1944**

One victory that MacDonald certainly scored while flying this Lightning (the second P-38 to carry the name *PUTT PUTT MARU*) was a Zeke on 8 June 1944, downed some 60 miles north-west of Manokwari Island. It was the custom in the 475th to have 432nd FS maintainers service Col MacDonald's P-38, but for some inexplicable reason this particular aircraft was looked after by the 433rd FS. It was reportedly written off during a routine flight from Biak during July or August 1944.

## 35

**P-38J-15 42-103921 of Lt Richard E West, 35th FS/8th FG, Owi, July 1944**

West claimed a Zeke and a 'Tony' on 16 June and 27 July respectively in a P-38J-15, although there are no records available to show that he used this machine. He had previously scored six kills flying P-40Ns with the 35th FS in 1943, and went on to score a further eight in the Lightning. West considered the P-38L to be the ultimate fighter in the Pacific, and named his last mount after his daughter Linda. West received this J-15 in early April 1944, and it may have been lost in a surprise Japanese air attack on Wakde two months later.

## 36

**P-38J-15 43-28831 of Maj Clifton Troxell, 35th FS/8th FG, Owi, July 1944**

Troxell scored two of his five victories flying a P-38G near Wewak in September 1943 – he had earlier claimed two Zeros in P-39s, and went on to make ace in a P-40N-5 on Boxing Day 1943. He lent this P-38 to Charles Lindbergh when the famed transatlantic flyer flew with the 35th FS in combat. The latter actually shot down an enemy aircraft whilst flying with the 475th FG soon after his visit to the 8th FG, an action which resulted in 475th boss 'Mac' MacDonald being recalled to the US for three months on disciplinary grounds!

## 37

**P-38L (serial unknown) of Maj Gerald Johnson, Deputy CO of the 49th FG, Biak, October 1944**

Johnson probably scored victories 12 and 13 (a 'Tojo' and an 'Oscar') in this fighter during a mission to Balikpapan on 14 October 1944. His combat style was also hard on machinery, and he used at least three P-38s between the end of 1944 and the spring of the following year.

## 38

**P-38L-1 44-23964 of Maj Dick Bong, Fifth Fighter Command, Tacloban, November 1944**

Bong definitely used this 8th FS L-1LO to score his last victories whilst attached to the 49th FG in November 1944. He claimed an 'Oscar' and two Zekes over Ormoc Bay on the 10th and 11th of the month respectively, thus taking his score to 36 – this fighter was later lost whilst being flown by another pilot on 28 November. Bong used 'Yellow 42' for just a month between the end of October and mid-November, yet managed to score six kills during this period. His last four victories came whilst flying a P-38L-1 from the 475th FG.

## 39

**P-38J-15 43-268?? of Lt John S Dunaway, 36th FS/8th FG, Morotai, November 1944**

Trained as a photo-recon pilot, Dunaway quickly requested a transfer to fighters when he ascertained that the Lightnings he was initially going to fly were unarmed! Six of his seven kills were claimed in a ten-day period in early November 1944 over the Philippines. His excellent run of success was abruptly stopped on the 22nd of the month when the wingtip of his P-38 caught a wave during a low strafing run over Halmaheras and he crashed into the water in Kaohe Bay, off Miti Island.

## 40

**P-38L-5 44-25930/*LIZZIE V* of Capt John E Purdy, 433rd FS/475th FG, Dulag, December 1944**

It is likely that Purdy scored the last of his seven kills in this fighter when he downed two Zeke Model 52s over Mindoro on 17 December 1944. *LIZZIE V* was hit by AA and subsequently written off in a crash-landing south of Malabang on 9 January 1945, Purdy being rescued soon after.

## 41

**P-38L-5 44-25327 of Capt Ferneley H Damstrom, 7th FS/49th FG, Tacloban, December 1944**

Damstrom scored eight victories between 2 November and 20 December 1944 before being killed in a take-off accident at Laong airfield, on northern Luzon, on 11 April 1945 – he was flying this P-38 at the time of his death.

## 42

**P-38L-5 44-25880/*LITTLE EVA* of Capt Calvin C Wire, CO of the 433rd FS/475th FG, Dulag, December 1944**

A seasoned P-38 veteran by the time he made CO of the 433rd in December 1944, Wire had scored his first victory with the squadron as early as 2 September 1943 when he claimed an 'Oscar', with another probably destroyed, flying P-38H-1 42-66539 over Wewak. His final claims (two 'Oscars') were downed off the west coast of Leyte on 19 November 1944.

## 43

**P-38J-15 42-104454 of Lt Zach Dean, 432nd FS/475th FG, Dobodura, January 1945**

Dean scored all seven of his confirmed kills flying H-models, and saw little aerial combat in this J-15. His crewchief, Sgt R Stidd, was extremely proud of each P-38 used by his pilot, dispensing loving care with every service of this gleaming Lightning. Dean was an unusually highly-strung pilot that demanded the very best from his groundcrewmen, and Stidd never failed to deliver.

## 44

**P-38L-5 44-25453/*GEORGIA BELLE*/*MARTHA* of Capt Joel Paris, 7th FS/49th FG, Lingayen, March 1945**

Having got a trio of kills in P-40Ns earlier in 1944, Paris scored a further six victories in P-38Ls – five of them over the Philippines, starting with a Ki-45 near Cebu City on 7 December 1944. His fifth P-38 victory took the form of a Zeke Model 52 downed over Clark Field on New Year's Day 1945, whilst his last kill (also a Zeke) was scored on a long-range mission over Hainan Island on 6 March 1945.

## 45

**P-38L-5 44-25471/*PUTT PUTT MARU* of Col Charles H MacDonald, CO of the 475th FG, Clark Field, March 1945**

'Mac' MacDonald scored his 27th, and last, aerial victory in this stunningly-marked L-5 on 13 February 1945 when he downed a 'Topsy' transport off the coast of Indo-China. The prop, fin and boom stripes reflect the three colours of the units that comprised MacDonald's command. He was rotated home in July, turning the 475th over to his loyal subordinate, Lt Col John Loisel.

## 46
### P-38L-5 44-25639/*Vickie* of Capt John 'Rabbit' Pietz, 431st FS/475th FG, Lingayen, April 1945

Pietz scored his six victories between November 1944 and March 1945, and it is likely that his final claim (a 'Tojo' on 28 March off the coast of Indo-China) was achieved in this L-5.

## 47
### P-38L-5 44-25863/*PEEWEE V* of Capt Ken Hart, 431st FS/475th FG, Lingayen, June 1945

Hart had claimed all eight of his kills by the time this L-5 was assigned to him in mid-1945. Note the unusual positioning of the 'Satan's Angels' group badge on the port radiator housing.

## 48
### P-38L-5 44-25673 of Lt Col Bill Harris, CO of the 18th FG, Zamboana, August 1945

This machine was the final mount of Lt Col Harris, who scored more victories (16) in the P-38 than any other pilot in the Thirteenth Air Force. He flew this L-5 from 5 August 1945 through to the end of the war just over a fortnight later.

# FIGURE PLATES

## 1

Lt 'Ailing Allen' Hill of the 80th FS/8th FG is seen at Finschhafen in January 1944. The hunting knife was considered an indispensable tool in surviving a bail out over the New Guinea jungle by a number of leading aces. Although a knife like this was optional, all pilots carried a sidearm, and there was much conjecture about the most useful gun to take aloft. Many preferred a six-shot .38 cal revolver as it was less prone to jamming when fired, or to rusting in the moist conditions of the tropics, whilst others (Hill included) swore by the heavy firepower and wearing comfort of a flat .45 semi-automatic pistol.

## 2

Twelve-kill ace Capt James 'Duckbutt' Watkins of the 49th FG – seen at Lingayen in March 1945 – is wearing the late-war one-piece flying overall that combined comfort with protection against the notoriously cold environs of the P-38 cockpit at altitude. Watkins earned his nickname thanks to the odd gait that he adopted when he walked from the briefing hut to his aircraft with his parachute pack strapped to his rear! The pipe was almost a permanent fixture in his mouth between sorties.

## 3

Maj Ed 'Porky' Cragg, CO of the 80th FS/8th FG, is seen at Finschhafen in December 1943 wearing standard issue lightweight khaki trousers, matched with a white T-shirt – he regularly flew without his uniform shirt. One of the difficulties in dressing for operational flights in the heat and humidity of the New Guinea climate was that the temperature cooled considerably at altitude – on average it fell 3° for every 1000 ft. Thus, 90° Fahrenheit at sea level dropped into freezing temperatures of around 30° at 20,000 ft. Cragg wore his RAF issue flying boots (perhaps acquired from an RAAF pilot?) to keep his feet warm at altitude, and on at least one mission was glad to have swapped his T-shirt for the standard issue item, for the long sleeves of the latter helped soak up the blood from a shrapnel wound to his arm. Note his Colt .45 semi-automatic pistol and the dinghy stored in the parachute harness on his back, the latter forming a cushion against the bare armour plate of the seat in his P-38.

## 4

Lt Col Robert Westbrook, Deputy CO of the 347th FG, is seen in full flying rig at Middleburg in September 1944. Aside from wearing a lightweight one-piece overall, he has an S-1 parachute harness, with associated raft and survival kit, strapped to his back, and is carrying his oxygen mask, leather helmet and goggles. Like most Lightning pilots in the South and Southwest Pacific, Westbrook is wearing gloves and boots more in an effort to stave off the cold and fight flying fatigue, rather than to protect him from a cockpit fire – P-38 pilots seemed not to be too concerned about the latter.

## 5

Lt Dick Bong of the 9th FS/49th FG is seen early on in his career at Dobodura in April 1943. This was his standard rig for much of his time in New Guinea, with the ubiquitous baseball cap being favoured over the more formal service hat – the khaki cap was a prized item amongst fighter pilots, who wore them to ward off the sun while on the ground. Note too that Bong is wearing gaiters with his regulation issue boots, the former having been all but removed from service by this stage in the war. The hunting knife in the scabbard on his waist had been personally acquired by Bong, although fortunately for him it saw more use on fishing trips to streams near to the group's Dobodura strip than as a potential aid in the event of him being forced down in the jungle.

## 6

Maj Tom McGuire, CO of the 431st FS/475th FG, is seen at Biak soon after completing a successful sortie in mid-October 1944. Like Westbrook, he too is in a one-piece lightweight overall (although this example lacks the lower leg map pockets), with an S-1 lifejacket draped over his chest. It was rare to catch the major wearing his flying helmet while on the ground, for he had trained his groundcrew to have his favourite battered (some even suggested 'disgraceful') service hat ready for donning as soon he had stepped out of his Lightning. Note that his helmet is minus goggles – for some inexplicable reason McGuire was seldom, if ever, photographed in a flying helmet with goggles attached.